The Listed Buildings
and
Other Principal Structures
at the
Royal Gunpowder Mills
Waltham Abbey

Les Tucker

ROYAL
GUNPOWDER
MILLS
Waltham Abbey

An Archive project of the Royal Gunpowder Mills

First Edition 2013

© Copyright 2013 Royal Gunpowder Mills

ISBN 978-1493561254

Published by

Royal Gunpowder Mills
Beaulieu Drive, Waltham Abbey, Essex, EN9 1JY
Registered Charity No. 1062968
www.royalgunpowdermills.com

Cover Illustrations

Top: Watercolour (RGM Archives WAI-1248-01) by Peter Jackson based on the 1735 engraving of the Waltham Abbey Mills published by J. Farmer; (RGM Archives WAI-0093-01).
Left side: Listed Building L135; (RGM Archives WAI-1585-02-02).
Right side top: Listed Building L136; (RGM Archives WAI-1585-03-02).
Right side bottom: Listed Building L157; (RGM Archives WAI-1585-03-02).

The Listed Buildings and Other Principal Structures at the Royal Gunpowder Mills Waltham Abbey

Les Tucker

History, Industrial Archaeology, Technology

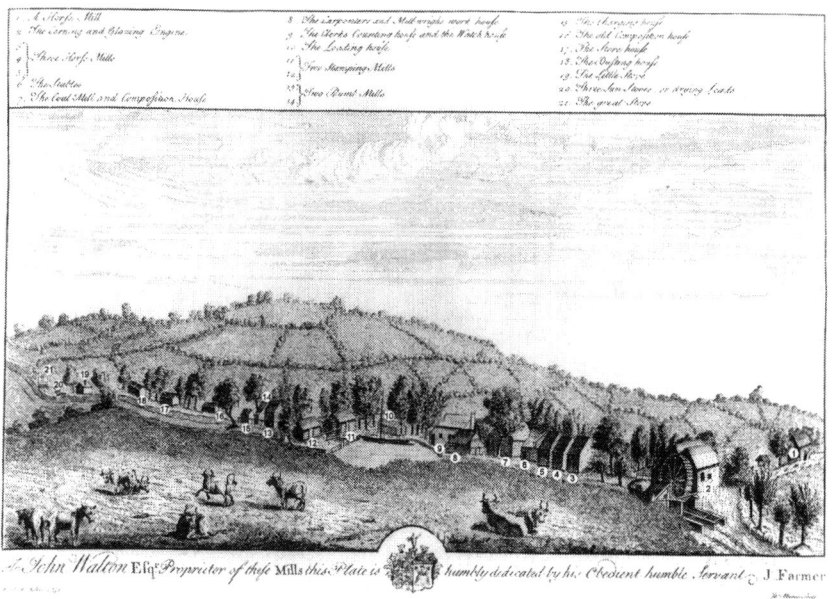

Fig.1 WAI-0093-01: Farmer engraving, 1735.

"... curious Gunpowder Mills, which supply the nation with great quantities of gunpowder, being esteemed the largest and compleatest Works in Great Britain."

(- John Farmer, History of the ancient town and once famous Abbey of Waltham from foundation to present time, 1735)

In an official report The Royal Gunpowder Mills Waltham Abbey were described as "the most important site for the history of explosives in Europe".

Many of the major world advances in gunpowder and explosive production using a range of technologies were made here, continuing into the later role of Research Centre, extending to rocket propellant.

The listed buildings are unique surviving structures spanning the range of this activity which was carried on for the Crown in conditions of secrecy for over 200 years.

This came to an end in 1991 when the Establishment's role was transferred to other centres and from 2001 for the first time this remarkable site was opened to the outside world.

Table of Contents

Acknowledgements

My thanks go to Brenda Buchanan for the Introduction, to Clive England for the Foreword and to Wayne Cocroft for the commentary on English Heritage listing.

Brenda's *The Old Establishment*, in the *Transactions of the Newcomen Society* of 1998 - 9, was essential to an understanding of the historical origins of the Mills and Wayne's *The Royal Gunpowder Factory, Waltham Abbey Essex, An RCHME Survey, 1993* was a fundamental information source.

Catherine Morton Lloyd kindly commented on the structure of the booklet.

My thanks to Ian MacFarlane for the layout, design and image presentation of this publication. Also for his contribution on Archive Information Technology in general, and particularly including his instigation and development of the RGM Document and Image Digital Archive.

The booklet drew extensively on the Waltham Abbey Archive, particularly the Waltham Abbey Special Collection of documents (WASC) and the Waltham Abbey Image Collection (WAI). These digitised collections provide a unique record of gunpowder, explosives and propellant production and research at Waltham Abbey and the wider arena from the 18th century to post WW2.

Thanks go to Richard Thomas for his work throughout on Archive collating and cataloguing and similarly to Michael Seymour for his work on image digitisation - both vital contributions to booklet writing and the wider Archive.

The Royal Gunpowder Mills acknowledge the generosity of the Gunpowder and Explosives History Group in sponsoring this booklet. The group was established in 1985 as the Gunpowder Mills Study Group to investigate all aspects of the manufacture of gunpowder. Later its interests expanded to include more modern explosives. In 2009 it became an e-group and donated its remaining funds to furthering the study of the explosives industry through supporting publications by the Royal Gunpowder Mills, where many successful meetings had been held. Back issues of the group's newsletters may be found at:

http://www.royalgunpowdermills.com/history-and-heritage/gehg/

Introduction

"Gunpowder, and the explosives and propellants which
followed it, provided a form of energy which changed the
world."

These words were written in 1998 in the introduction to the first
leaflet to serve as a guide to this site of exceptional importance,
for which I wrote the text and Wayne Cocroft of English Heritage
contributed the maps and photographs. I make no apology for
repeating them because this general observation forms a suitable
background to Les Tucker's highly detailed account of *The Listed
Buildings and Other Principal Structures at the Royal
Gunpowder Mills Waltham Abbey,* placing his welcome study in
a broad perspective.

From their purchase by the Crown in 1787 to their de-
commissioning in 1991, the Waltham Abbey Royal Gunpowder
Mills remained in government hands, becoming over the years an
explosives factory and then a research centre. They continued in
a state of such closely-guarded secrecy that even in May 1992,
arriving for an arranged meeting of the Gunpowder Mills Study
Group, we were waved in with the observation that our car
number had already been noted - registered we surmised when
we arrived early, loitered at the gate, and then went off to fill in
time by exploring the town. There was already much interest in
the future of the site, especially in the local area, as a southern
section had already been sold for housing and light industrial and
warehousing development in the 1980s. Was the same to happen
to the northern section, to provide funds for an always hard-
pressed Ministry of Defence? Mindful of what would be lost if
this site of such historical significance was sold for commercial
purposes, the GMSG decided that we must ask for a thorough-

going survey to be made. Fortunately, as a Royal Commissioner my husband Angus Buchanan was well-placed to put this request to the Royal Commission on the Historical Monuments of England, who acted with commendable speed by sending in a team to undertake the survey of this large site of great complexity, requiring desk-research as well as practical skills of investigation both above and below ground. The effective leader was Wayne Cocroft, but many professionals became involved in this task which was to provide the evidence for the naming of twenty one structures as Listed Buildings and the designation of a large area as a Scheduled Ancient Monument. This splendid work by the RCHME (now incorporated in English Heritage) has provided a firm footing from which later research may be developed.

But at the same time as the practical evidence was being gathered, the written evidence, especially the documentary material and plans, was being dispersed because the process of de-contamination was making it impossible for it to be kept on the site. The work in recent years of Les Tucker and his colleagues (many with an excellent familiarity with the site through having worked there) in the sorting and cataloguing of archival material is much to be praised. So also is the new venture now underway, aiming to produce books of manageable size and detail that will introduce visitors to significant aspects of the site. The Royal Gunpowder Mills badly need such a series. So far Richard Thomas' account of *The Waterways of the Royal Gunpowder Mills* has been published, followed by his *The Explosions at the Royal Gunpowder Mills* and Peter Blake's *Military Superintendents of the Royal Gunpowder Mills*. *The Workforce of the Royal Gunpowder Mills:1787-1841* and *Workforce Worthies of the Royal Gunpowder Mills* by Derek Armes and Sandra Taylor have been published, to be followed by Les Tucker's study of *The Listed Buildings and Other Principal Structures at the Royal Gunpowder Mills*.

The historical importance of this gunpowder mills site with its roots going back to the 1660s, and its continuity of use over many years and through various technological developments, makes it probably the most significant of those surviving today.

We came close to losing it. Now however, we have the opportunity to build a series of publications to match the practical work of archaeology and survey undertaken in the earliest days of the rescue of this fascinating place.

Brenda Buchanan
Foundation Trustee, 1997-2007, the nominee of the Science Museum

The Royal Gunpowder Mills - A Protected Place

Internationally, the Royal Gunpowder Mills is amongst a handful of places associated with the manufacture of explosives dating back many centuries which have subsequently been preserved and opened to the public. Gunpowder production began on the site in the 1660s and after the Crown acquired it in 1787 it became one of the world's most important centres for the understanding and manufacture of gunpowder. A century later most of the factory was converted for the manufacture of chemical explosives and set standards that were emulated at home and abroad. Explosives manufacture ceased during the Second World War and after 1945 the site became the country's most important explosives research centre until its closure in 1991.

The national significance of the Royal Gunpowder Mills is recognised through the legal protection given to many of its buildings and archaeological remains. The earliest water-powered mills were located along Millhead Stream and their sites to either side fall within the Scheduled Monument. This extends northwards for 38 hectares to embrace one of the largest scheduled industrial monuments in the country. The local authority also recognises the importance of the site through a large Conservation Area, which covers most of the former factory. Unique remains include oval-shaped brick blast protection walls, built during the Napoleonic Wars at the beginning of the 19th century. The remains of cordite production, a propellant explosive that contained nitroglycerine and guncotton, dominate the area, including two nitroglycerine works and rows of guncotton drying stoves. The earliest listed buildings on the site date from the 1780s when the Crown first acquired the site. These include Walton's House, a purpose built office for the government's clerks. Opposite to this are the earliest processing buildings on the site, the Mixing House and Saltpetre Melting House, both were involved in the preparation of ingredients and are listed as Grade II*. Although utilitarian structures, they are fine examples of military buildings of this date.

The long range of Victorian steam-powered gunpowder mills dominates the southern part of the site. Internationally, these mills built between 1861 and 1889, are the most architecturally distinguished gunpowder mills. The power houses of the roughly contemporary French mills at Sevran Livry, near Paris, are housed in impressive buildings, but are more dispersed and in consequence lack the visual impact of the Waltham Mills. While the royal Prussian gunpowder mills at Spandau were largely cleared after the First World War and few traces now remain. The importance of Waltham Abbey's steam-powered mills are reflected in their high listing grades. One is designated at Grade 1 and all but one of the remainder are listed at Grade II*. Nationally, only about 8% of all listed buildings are protected at these higher grades.

This booklet is an excellent introduction to the Royal Gunpowder Mills listed buildings - structures that once housed state of the art technology designed to supply the armed forces with the most up-to-date explosives.

Wayne Cocroft
Senior Investigator
English Heritage

Foreword

I first came to the Gunpowder Mills on a wet and gloomy autumnal day in 1997.

Over the succeeding months of surveying and planning, I came to know the site and its buildings in even greater detail and the more time that I spent there the more fascinated I became with the stories of the site and of the people who had worked there. The buildings are interesting in their own right, exhibiting many interesting details of design and construction, but it is the way in which they are so closely intertwined with the development of explosives, and of their manufacturing processes, which adds an additional dimension, and makes the whole site so remarkable. It is a story which includes experimentation, industrial production, dangerous materials, risk, secrecy, security and the demands of war. It should also be remembered that however the site appears today, it was for hundreds of years a nationally important, high tech, high security manufacturing and research facility which supported the British military machine from gunpowder through to the Blue Streak missile. In their day, gunpowder and later, cordite and nitroglycerine were the keys to military warfare and national security.

The development and production of ever more powerful explosives was just as much an 'arms race' as that to develop the atomic bomb in the 20th century. The processes were at the cutting edge of technology, as were the successive power sources which operated the equipment.

Because of its secrecy and the physical isolation caused by its location, the site was self-contained, with its own power station, railway, road and canal systems.

The design of the buildings, and indeed the whole layout of the site, can only be fully understood in the context of the very real dangers involved in the manufacturing processes. How can one make sense of felt covered external walls, elephant hide floor coverings fixed with copper nails, bare timber board roofs and canvas lined walls without understanding the catastrophic consequences of a single spark!

Some of the buildings have been adapted and re-used over time, adding further layers to their histories, Others were so process-specific that they were incapable of any other use and remain much as they were when they were first constructed and then later abandoned. Minimising the risk of explosions and minimising the damage caused by explosions were the two key factors in the designs of the majority of the buildings. - the former epitomised by the use of non-sparking materials (wood, copper, canvas, felt) and the strict separation between 'clean' and 'dirty' areas and the latter by the use of massive structures to protect adjacent areas and equipment, by the use of flimsy structures to allow an escape from explosive forces and minimise dangerous debris, and by the use of remote boiler and engine houses with large separation between buildings. This strange mixture of the massive and ephemeral has a major effect on the current appearance of the buildings, with a much higher survival rate among the former. This is a continuing process which can only be slowed by constant maintenance - a tremendous task bearing in mind the number of buildings and structures.

There is a large amount to see and understand from these buildings, in terms of both the processes which they contained and the lives of the people who worked in them. The buildings range from structures big enough to be landscape features (the Nitrator - E2) to the merely monumental (concrete traverses) to the small and human scale (earth closets). Some are strange - the experimental concrete structure of the Quinan Stove, and the use of an exposed structural timber frame for the otherwise conventional brick - clad laboratory at the north - west corner of Queen's Mead. Some structures have to be imagined, such as the missing elevated small - gauge railway which ran along the Queen's Mead, linking the elevated doors of the incorporating mills and magazines.

The site can also be enjoyed simply as a fascinating 'lost world' of buildings set within a vast and isolated forest, itself a product of the trees first planted to make charcoal for the manufacture of gunpowder and which has now given birth to its own unique ecosystem. A remarkable and unique site with an important place in the secret history of Britain - and this booklet is a perfect introduction!

Clive England
Lead Architect

The History of Gunpowder and Propellants

An explosion is a process of rapidly accelerated combustion accompanied by the release of a large amount of heat and gases. A basic form of combustion is fire. Combustion requires a supply of oxygen and fuel. For around 600 years gunpowder was the only product which combined oxygen and fuel to produce, with a suitable ignitor, an explosive effect.

The three ingredients of gunpowder were naturally occurring - the oxygen provider was saltpetre (potassium nitrate), the fuel was charcoal and sulphur helped to bind the other materials together and speeded up ignition.

There is no totally definitive account of how gunpowder came about. The most likely scenario points to China. Saltpetre was used by Chinese cooks and possibly by accident in cooking it was known that it could be ignited to produce a flaring effect. This in its turn was used for religious purposes to drive off evil spirits. It also was used by Chinese alchemists in their never ending quest to discover a method of making gold and other experiments. At some point in these experiments it was discovered that when combined with charcoal it produced a stronger burning effect together with noise and smoke, all important in religious practice and also in festivals, generally in the form of fireworks. Finally in the 10th century AD Taoist chemists stumbled across the fact that the effect was enhanced by the addition of sulphur, creating a rudimentary form of gunpowder.

The Chinese called it *huo yao* - 'fire drug'.

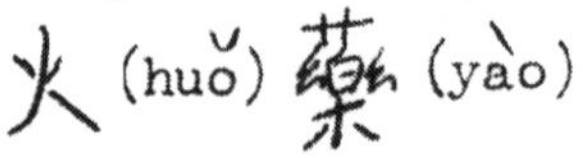

火 (huǒ) 藥 (yào)

Fig. 2 WAI-0605-01: Chinese characters for gunpowder.

16

Another important element in Chinese society, the generals, took a keen interest. Chinese warfare had always had an incendiary element and the new material lent itself to the development of devices which propelled fiery projectiles at the enemy. At first the projectiles were attached to long sticks 'fire lances' then gradually means were found to fire greater distances from bamboo tubes. The tubes were later strengthened with iron - the first guns. By the 13th century the Chinese had progressed to totally iron guns.

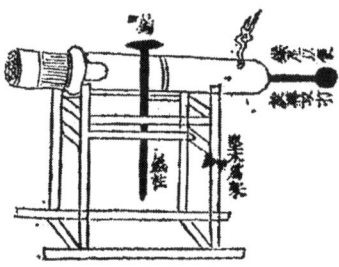

Fig. 3 WAI-0481- 03: Frame Mounted Fire Lance.

The Chinese had extensive trading links with the Arabs and probably via contact with Arab traders knowledge of the new technology came to North Africa and Europe. The English first used guns at the Battle of Crécy in 1346 (Fig. 4). It is not an exaggeration to say that gunpowder changed everything. The bastion of the feudal power of the knights was the castle. For the first time the means were available to demolish these bastions and with it feudal power, opening the way to a new structure of society.

In time ways were discovered of applying the power of gunpowder to civil use - in mining, quarrying, tunnelling and infrastructure development of all kinds, first the canals and roads then the railways, harbours and so on. The industrialisation of the

19th century would not have been possible without gunpowder's ability to shift literally mountains of earth and rock.

Fig. 4 WAI-1644-01: English Gun used at the Battle of Crécy in 1346.

During their operation, the Royal Gunpowder Mills passed through three main areas of activity - manufacture of natural based gunpowder, then chemically based cordite, guncotton, the high explosive RDX and the booster explosive tetryl and finally a research phase, with rocket propellant and specialised material research and manufacture coming to the fore alongside continuing explosive research. Many of the buildings survive today because they were converted and reused throughout the eighteenth and nineteenth centuries, in fact up until the site closed in 1991. The twenty one buildings listed by English Heritage reflect this historical process (see list in Appendix).

The foundation of gunpowder manufacture at Waltham Abbey was a water driven mill originally employed for cloth fulling - cleaning, shrinking and thickening. The water source was what came to be known as the Millhead Stream. In common with many water mills this mill changed its production in line with changes in demand. Thus by the 1650s it had become an 'oyle' mill, producing oils from vegetable material for purposes such as leather processing. The expansion of trade routes and the need to protect them and increasing rivalry between nation states had led to an increasing demand for gunpowder and in 1665 the mill was converted to gunpowder production, passing into the hands of the Walton family at the beginning of the 18th century. The Waltons built the business expanding north up the Millhead Stream to the point where it became a significant manufacturing entity, one of the most important in the country at that time. Its importance as a supplier to the Government led to its purchase for the Crown in 1787.

The listed buildings reflect the span of the Mills history from the original buildings of 1787 to the steam age from mid 19th century, the development of hydraulic and electric power and the progress of safety provision. They stand as the most important buildings of a remarkable technological progression, ushering in the latest steam technology, changing the character and scale of production, later as part of a system applying hydraulic technology on a large scale, then as a leader in the application of the new organic chemistry to production on an industrial scale in the shape of guncotton and cordite, and finally scientific research employing the most advanced techniques. The incorporating mills dominated and still dominate the Establishment, physically and historically, and therefore they are taken as the lead topic in the first three chapters of this monograph.

By 1888 Waltham Abbey had 40 steam powered incorporating mills, combined with iron edge runners, producing a substantial increase in productivity. In previous years a pair of water-turned stone runners could produce 660 barrels of cannon powder or 330 barrels of small arms powder. The comparable figures for steam driven iron runners were 990 and 473 respectively. The cumulative repetition of style and scale of these mill buildings creates overall an impressive architectural grouping. There is a strong symmetry lending an impression of power and at the same time, large scale efficient industrial organisation. Beyond the architectural and technological, the range of these mills, until recently cloaked in secrecy, deserves now to be known as a monument to a time when amazingly a small island nation on the fringes of Europe projected its power and influence to bring Pax Britannica to a major part of the globe - still a subject generating debate.

Fig. 5 WAI-0448-02: Mid 19[th]C Overhead Drive Gunpowder Incorporating Mill. (Illustrated London News, 11.11.1854)

The Group C Mills design proved to be eminently successful and were the template for subsequent gunpowder incorporating mills built at Waltham Abbey. Reflecting its significance, Group C is the most important grouping surviving on site and has received an English Heritage Grade 1 listing.

Having introduced a major change in power technology in the mid 19th century, at the end of that century the Mills, over a very short space of time, had to manage a fundamental change in the technology and manufacturing processes of its main product, from a basis of natural ingredients - saltpetre, sulphur, charcoal, for gunpowder to guncotton and nitroglycerine for cordite. The list of the tasks was daunting - building of new unfamiliar plant; conversion of old plant; installing of unfamiliar machinery; learning of new processes; staff to be retrained; new materials handling and safety procedures; new laboratory and testing procedures. That all this was achieved and the high quality standards of Waltham Abbey gunpowder perpetuated in the new material was impressive indeed.

Messrs. Abel, Dewar and Dupre, scientists of the late Victorian era, created a classic product in cordite. It has been called "the most famous smokeless powder of all". It was robust, reliable, safe to handle, widely adaptable to changes in specification, susceptible to rigorous quality control. In a remarkable feat of technological longevity it remained for over 50 years of the 20th century the key British military propellant. In a period which included two World Wars of national survival and beyond it unfailingly performed in every action fought - from massive set piece battles to the smallest skirmish. The place of cordite in the history of British technology is assured as a key chemical element in national defence and the Mills at Waltham Abbey stand as the origin, major supplier and technical developer of this key material for over half a century.

In the wider industrial arena, textile dyes and explosives, civil and military, were the two lead areas of the development of organic chemistry applied on an industrial scale - ultimately adding to the economy a whole new organic chemistry based industry producing a vast range of products from the original dyes and explosives to pharmaceuticals, medical drugs, photographic materials, perfumery, paints and so on.

As in the technical field, the Factory was also in the forefront of safety development which fully reflected and was in advance of explosives legislation.

Fig. 6 WAI-0475-01: Sir Frederick Abel KCB, FRS. First Chemical Advisor to the War Department and a key figure in the development of organic chemistry applied to the industrial production of explosives.

The rush of the Industrial Revolution and beyond and the pressures of competition had meant that Victorian industry placed safety far down the list of priorities. The Mills attention to safety was part of the long climb to better and safer working conditions which took place in industry generally.

The Royal Gunpowder Mills were recognised as one of the foremost centres of gunpowder and explosives production and expertise in the world. After the Second World War, the Research and Development Establishment carried on this expertise in the field of chemically based scientific research into explosives and rocketry propellant. Its research projects were leading edge in an era when the vision of a high - tech Britain was reflected in many defence products and it was recognised as a world class organisation.

Fig. 7 WAI-1529-01: Launch of Skylark Rocket. Very successful launch vehicle for space research with motor using plastic propellant developed at Waltham Abbey, c. 1957.

The Listed Incorporating Mills - The Era of Steam Produced Gunpowder: 1857 - 1897

"The Spirit of Artillery has been bridled as it never was before, and rendered much more manageable."

(From: *Gunpowder Considered as the Spirit of Artillery* - A paper read by Col. C. B. Brackenbury to the Royal United Service Institute, 28th February 1884.)

In the 1780s a debate arose within the Government as to the merits of sourcing the entire gunpowder requirement of the Forces from private producers as opposed to the Government owned mills at Faversham. The visionary military technocrat Major, later Lt. General Sir, William Congreve, then the Deputy Comptroller of the Royal Laboratory, advanced an opposing view based on considerations of security of supply, economy and the opportunity to create Government controlled standards of quality and performance which would act as a check on the private contractors retained to supplement Government produced material. Congreve's view prevailed. Faversham was retained and the policy was extended to approve expansion of Government facilities by purchase of the mills at Waltham Abbey owned by the Walton family. This was done in 1787 for the sum of £10000, creating the first 'nationalised' industry and, after extensive refurbishment to Congreve's exacting standards, 200 years of explosive and propellant production and research for the Crown commenced at the now Royal Gunpowder Mills Waltham Abbey.

The Government had acquired an establishment which was by the standards of the day a major industrial enterprise, already by the

1730s as the Figure 1 engraving shows a fully integrated power driven production centre which would employ a skilled and disciplined work force. If the process later called the Industrial Revolution very broadly could be taken to have commenced around the 1750s the Mills were thus well in the van and in fact were a precursor, deserving a place in the country's economic history.

Fig. 8 WAI-0111-02: Lt. General Sir William Congreve 1st Baronet, Comptroller of the Royal Laboratory, late 18th century. Visionary soldier-technologist. (Philip de Loutherbourg,RA., British Museum)

Fig. 9 WAI-0633-01: Royal Laboratory Woolwich (built 1694-1696) 1735. (Maritime Museum Greenwich)

The Old Establishment - Water Power

At that time the mills were water and horse powered. A canal system provided water both to drive the mills and provide a safe means of transport of the products around and out of the site, linking into the River Thames via the Lee Navigation to the magazines at Woolwich and Purfleet.

The original water driven mills - 'The Old Establishment' lay along the Millhead Stream on the Mills western boundary running from the north of the site to the Millhead - the substantial brick remains of which can be seen north of the 1787 buildings (Fig. 12), and on to the Old River Lea.

The linear configuration of the mills can be clearly seen on the Farmer 1735 engraving. This line is closely paralleled on the east by today's Long Walk.

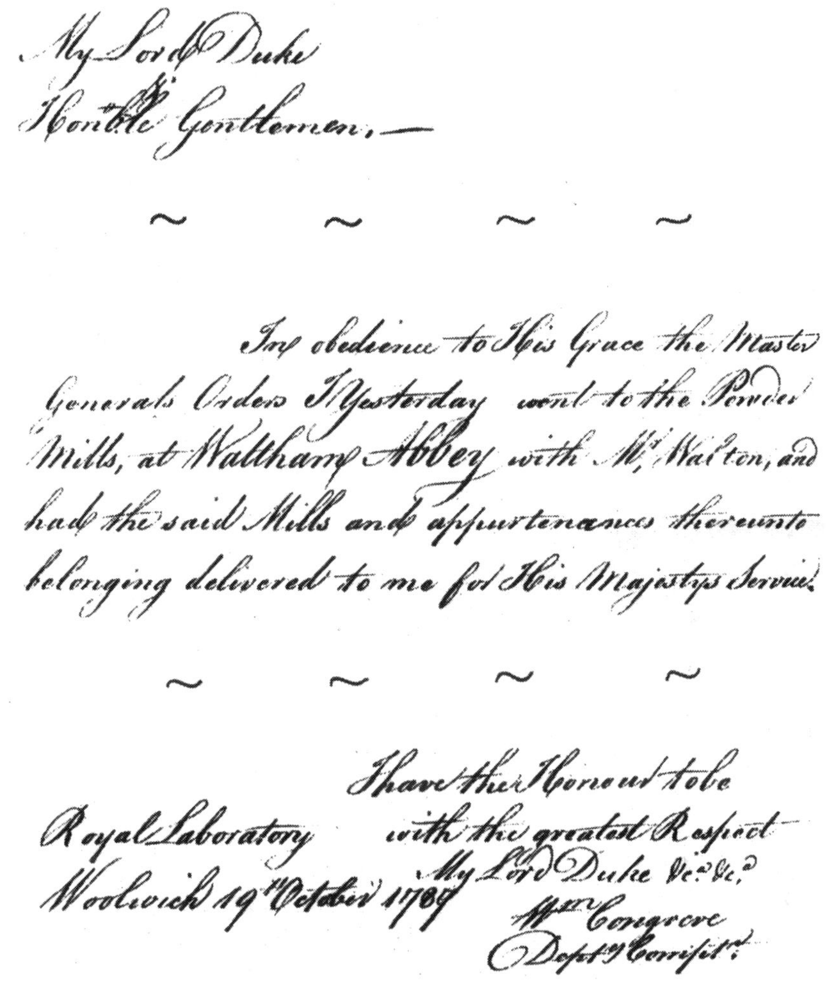

My Lord & Duke

Honble Gentlemen,—

~   ~   ~   ~

In obedience to His Grace the Master Generals Orders I Yesterday went to the Powder Mills, at Waltham Abbey with Mr. Walton, and had the said Mills and appurtenances thereunto belonging delivered to me for His Majestys Service.

~   ~   ~   ~

Royal Laboratory
Woolwich 19th October 1787

I have the Honour to be with the greatest Respect My Lord Duke &c &c

Wm Congreve
Depty Comptlr

Fig. 10 WAI-0595-01: Letter from William Congreve, then Major, Deputy Comptroller of the Royal Laboratory, to the Duke of Richmond, Master General of Ordnance, notifying takeover of the Mills from John Walton 19th October 1787.

27

Fig. 11 WAI-0080-01: The Millhead in the 1930s.

Fig. 12 WAI-1664-01: The Millhead in 2012.

It is believed that the building which can be seen at the north (top) of Figure 13 is building 159. This is located across the leat on the west side of the Long Walk roughly in line with L153 Group D mills across to the east on Queens Mead. 159 was a dusting house and is of particular historical significance as it is believed it was the only water driven building on the Millhead which performed the same function throughout the life of the mills and of which there are surviving surface elements - wheel pit, water flow ironwork, machine mounting block, traverse.

None of the original Millhead Stream water-powered incorporating mill buildings have survived. The following is a progression of images from mid 19th century through to the end of their life.

Fig. 13 WAI-0448-01: Mills and Powder Boat on the Millhead Stream, 1854. Until 1945 internal transport in the Factory was by water in two craft types, man hauled open punts or covered boats, the latter as seen in the image. (The Illustrated London News, 11.11.1854)

Fig. 14 WAI-0102-05: Millhead Stream, 1899. The Mills and Powder Boats on the Millhead. (Navy and Army Illustrated, 14.10.1899)

Fig. 15 WAI-0041-04: Millhead Stream, 1919. No.4 Incorporating Mill on left, No.2 on right. (Lt. E. L. Blee)

Fig. 16 WAI-0355-01: Derelict Mills on the Millhead, 1950s.

The Manufacture of Gunpowder at RGPF Waltham Abbey

The manufacture of gunpowder, a combination of three natural products - saltpetre, sulphur and charcoal, is a batch production process in which the material passes through a series of operations each adding an aspect of quality until the final product is achieved:

1. Initial preparation of ingredients - Saltpetre is refined. Charcoal is ground in a mill and sieved. Sulphur is refined and ground.

2. Mixing - Ingredients are weighed in standard British propellant proportions - Saltpetre 75 Charcoal 15 Sulphur 10 and mixed in mixing machine to produce 'Green Charge'.

Fig. 17 WAI-0101-02: Saltpetre Refinery. (Strand Magazine, Vol. IX, 1895)

Fig. 18 WAI-0101-05: Cylinder Charcoal Making. (Strand Magazine, Vol. IX, 1895)

Fig. 19 WAI-0101-03: Sulphur Refinery. (Strand Magazine, Vol. IX, 1895)

Fig. 20 WAI-0261-02: Ingredient Mixing. (Farmer Collection)

Fig. 21 WAI-0101-07: Incorporating Mill. (Strand Magazine, Vol. IX, 1895)

3. Incorporation - The green charge is incorporated, i.e. finely ground and pulverised by two asymmetric vertical revolving 'edge runners' (stones or later iron shod stone or iron) in the incorporating mill, to produce as intimate a combination as possible - fundamental to gunpowder quality - 'Mill Cake'.

Fig. 22 WAI-0443-72: Breaking Down Machine.

4. Breaking Down - The mill cake is broken down into powder by passing through a series of grooved rollers prior to pressing - 'Meal'.

5. Pressing - The meal is compressed in an Hydraulic Press to produce 'Press Cake'. Pressing increases density producing increased power and lessening susceptibility to breaking up in transport and moisture absorption. (For Pebble Powders the press cake goes directly to the cutting machine - see below.)

6. Granulating (Corning) - press cake rendered into grains of various shapes and sizes - 'Foul Grain', by passing through a series of toothed rollers allowing closer match to type of weapon employed, further increasing efficiency and power.

Fig. 23 WAI-0443-61: Gunpowder Press.

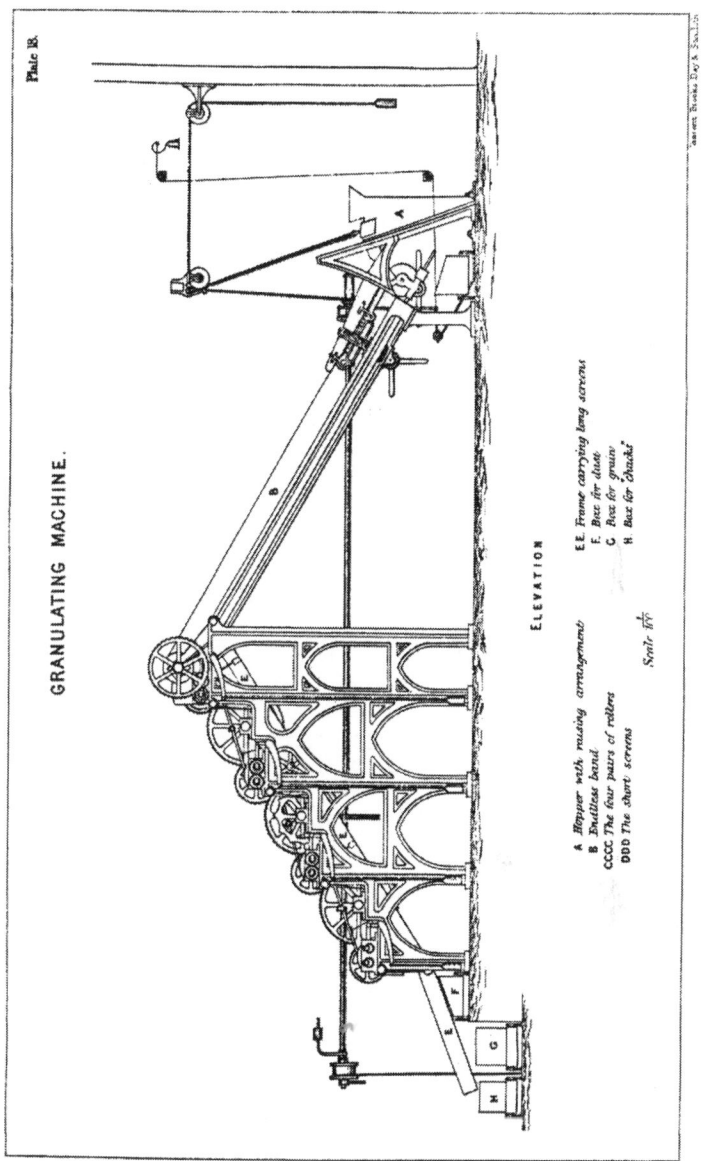

Fig. 24 WAI-0181-18: Granulating (Corning) Machine. (A Handbook of the Manufacture and Proof of Gunpowder as carried on at the Royal Gunpowder Factory Waltham Abbey, Capt. F. M. Smith RA, 1870)

Fig. 25 WAI-0443-74: Granulating (Corning) Machine.

7. Dusting - Foul grain has corners and carries some dust, both impeding performance and increasing possibility of moisture absorption. This particularly affects fine grain small arms powders. Dust is removed by tumbling these grains in a sloping reel (a fine mesh canvas over a wooden frame) in the Dusting House, producing rounded grains for glazing, with surplus dust collected for re processing. (For Pellet Powder and later Prism Powder the grain goes from the slope reel to a hydraulic moulding machine - see below.)

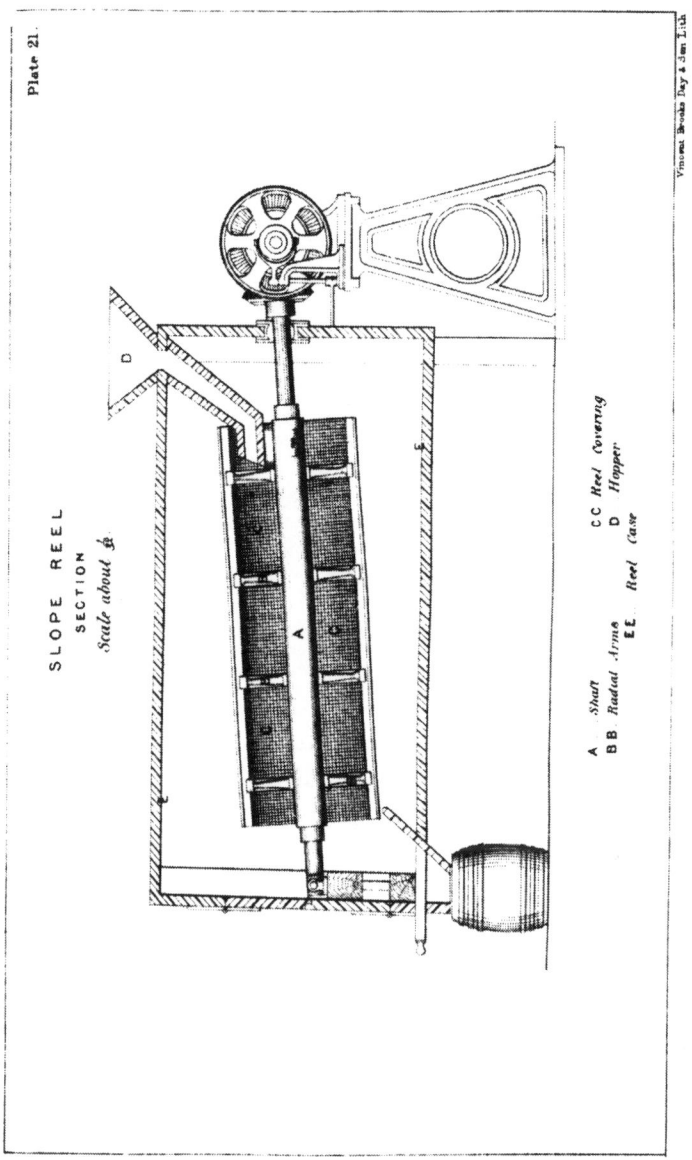

Fig. 26 WAI-0181-21: Dusting Reel. (A Handbook of the Manufacture and Proof of Gunpowder as carried on at the Royal Gunpowder Factory Waltham Abbey, Capt. F. M. Smith RA, 1870)

Fig. 27 WAI-0261-03: Glazing Barrels. (Farmer Collection)

Fig. 28 WAI-1590-01: Steam Stove. (Photograph 1993)

40

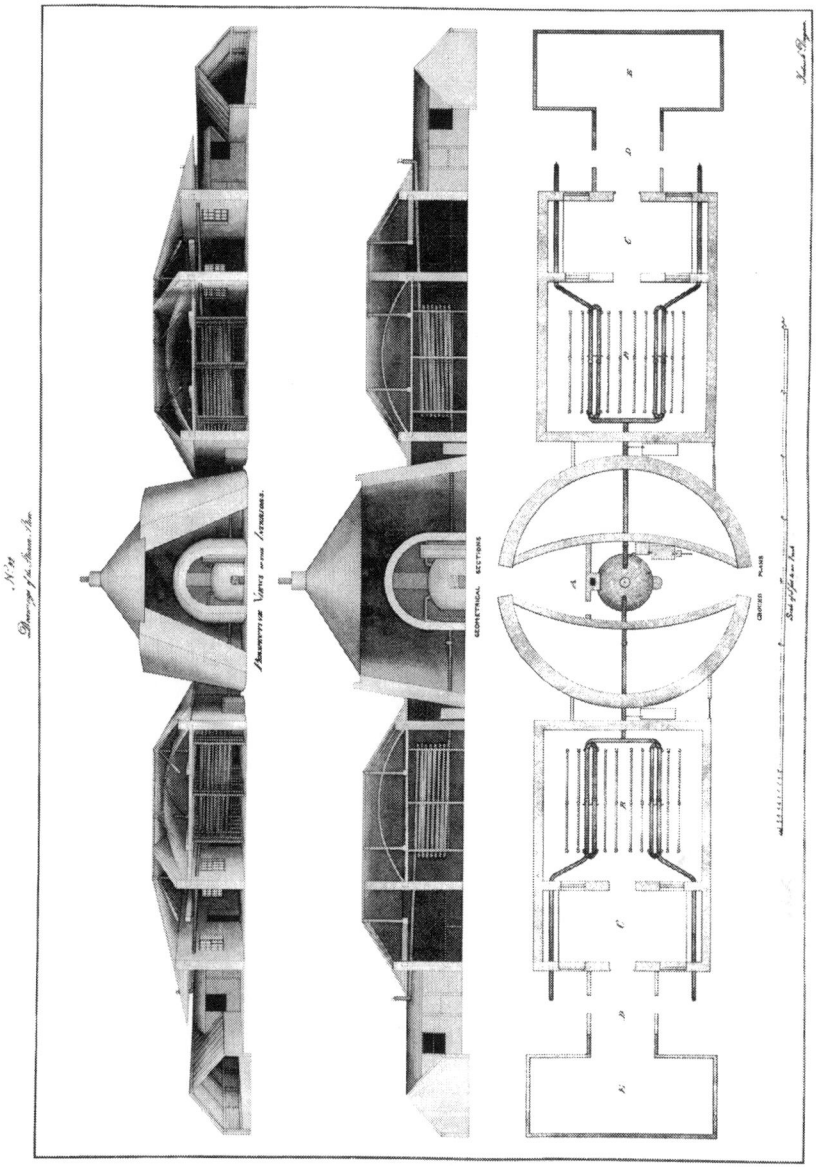

Fig. 29 WAI-0479-22: Steam Stove drawings. (A Treatise on Gunpowder, Frederick Drayson, 1830)

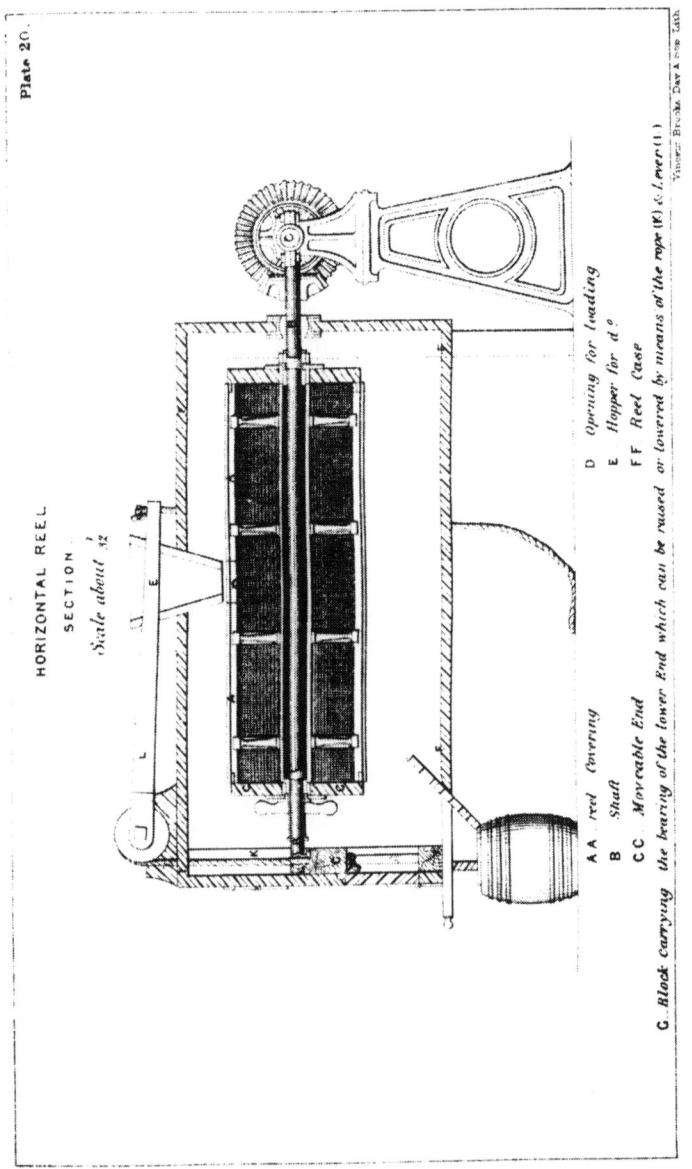

Fig. 30 WAI-0181-20: Finishing Reel. (A Handbook of the Manufacture and Proof of Gunpowder as carried on at the Royal Gunpowder Factory Waltham Abbey, Capt. F. M. Smith RA, 1870)

8. Glazing - All grains are tumbled together in a revolving wooden drum. In the case of larger grains graphite is added. The friction and heat generated imparts a glazed hardened surface, moderating ignition, lessening possibility of damage to guns and reducing the possibility of further dust formation.

9. Stoving (Drying) - Moisture is removed from grains by loading in trays racks and drying in heated drying room (stove), earlier by heat from a domed 'gloom stove' built into side wall with heat from rear of stove passing into drying room and later by steam pipes in the drying room served by a separate boiler house.

10. Finishing - A final dust removal. 'Finishing' is carried out by revolving in horizontal reels. This process also imparts a final glaze.

11. Blending - The finished granulated material contains grains of varying size. In order to obtain predictability and uniformity of performance, batches of finished material are blended together producing batches of 100 - 200 barrels of uniform quality.

Fig. 31 WAI-0601-04: Mortar Eprouvette.

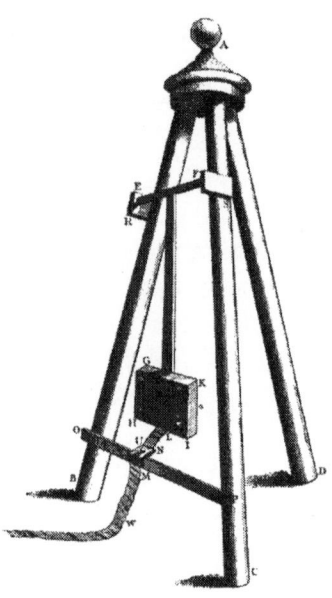

Fig. 32 WAI-0593-02: Ballistic Pendulum Eprouvette. (New Principles of Gunnery, B. Robins, 1805)

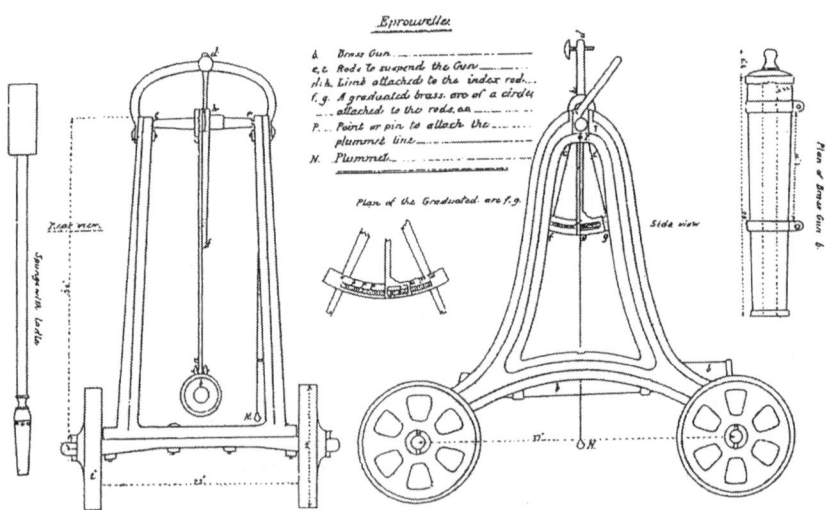

Fig. 33 WAI-1647-01: Ballistic Pendulum Eprouvette. (Small Arms of the East India Company 1600-1856, Vol. III, D. F. Harding, 1999)

12. Testing - Batches are proved, tested, for ballistic performance in eprouvettes for:

1. range - mortar eprouvette
2. penetration - measured by distance penetrated in series of planks
3. muzzle velocity - speed at which projectile leaves the barrel - ballistic pendulum eprouvette

13. Packing - Gunpowder is packed in oak barrels holding 100 lbs (except pebble 125 lbs.) Each barrel is marked with:

1. 'POWDER'
2. Quantity in barrel (weight in pounds)
3. Maker's name (either Waltham Abbey or private supplier)
4. Description of powder
5. Date of stoving, number of barrels in stoving, number of the barrel
6. Number of LOT
7. Tare (TR - weight in pounds) of barrel

Fig. 34 WAI-1095-01: Waltham Abbey Barrel Markings. (Ms. H. Maisey)

Fig. 35 WAI-0321-01: The Turnham Family - generations of coopers and barrel makers at Waltham Abbey.

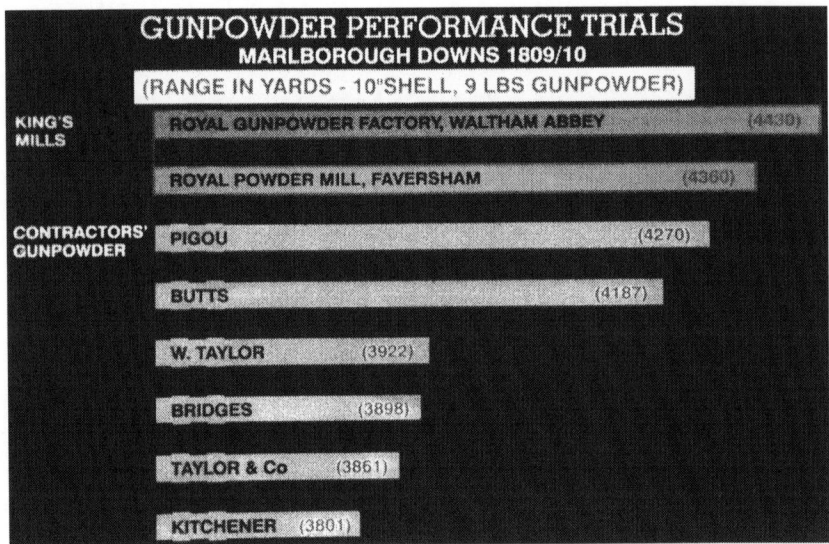

Fig. 36 WAI-0571-01: Marlborough Downs Performance Results, 1810 -1811.

Congreve's policy was amply vindicated. Figure 36 showing the results of range performance trials over 1809 - 1810 of Waltham Abbey and outside contractor material illustrates the superiority of Waltham Abbey. Private contractors still had some way to go but the example of Waltham Abbey undoubtedly spurred their efforts. In 1828 an artillery manual stated that between 1775 and 1828 improvements had resulted in British gunpowder almost doubling its strength.

By the mid 19th century Britain was approaching a zenith of imperial power, with its influence and territorial control extending over the globe. However a painful lesson was learned when Russian influence was confronted in the Crimean War 1854-1856. The War revealed almost catastrophic deficiencies in British organisation and supply of military materiel. This prompted considerable Government expenditure on new facilities.

New Mills, New Power Source - Steam

At Waltham Abbey this was reflected in an extensive building programme, including new gunpowder incorporating mills. For the first time the Mills used steam as the power source. The first group completed was Group A in 1857 with succeeding Groups up to 1888. Groups A and B were demolished (although the Engine House and Mechanics Shop - L168 and Boiler House - L176 of Group A survive and are listed). The balance - Groups C, D, E, F, G - comprise the present Listed Incorporating Mills.

Group	C	D	E	F	G
Built	1861	1867	1869[1]	1878	1888
Listing Grade	1	2*	2*	2	2*
Post WW2 Building No.	L157	L153	L149	L145	L148
			[1]Converted to gunpowder incorporation in 1878		

Looking across Queens Mead, the gleaming new mills must have presented a startling contrast to the venerable shed like structures of the old mills on the Millhead Stream, which nevertheless continued operating producing gunpowder for fuzes until the last mill ceased working at the end of 1940 (see Chapter 3).

The move to steam at the Waltham Abbey mills was a microcosm of the Industrial Revolution reflecting the developments which took place over the whole industrial spectrum:

- In adoption of a new power technology - replacement of water power by steam.
- In location - built on open land to the east of the Millhead Stream. The use of steam power freed the Mills from the need to locate in immediate proximity to a water power source.
- In configuration of the power train - underfloor in contrast to the overhead gearing of the water driven Millhead mills. The rotative steam engine made possible a more direct drive from an underfloor central shaft. This also had the advantage of protecting the material on the incorporating mill bed from pieces of material which might have dropped on to it from overhead gearing.
- Wood replaced by iron in machinery, gearing, etc., and employed in the steam engine, etc.

- Instead of wooden mills constructed by millwrights on site, iron machinery, etc., produced in factories for assembly on site.
- Steam power made possible the building of larger production units constructed of brick enabling installation of larger production units.

By the early 1780s James Watt had successfully developed and patented a reliable method of converting the 'to and fro' motion of the steam piston to rotative motion - one of the pillars of the Industrial Revolution. Not until more than half a century later was the new power source introduced to the Mills. On the face of it this seems extremely late in the day, bearing in mind that they had been in the van of the Revolution as a complete factory system. Part of this could be ascribed to innate conservatism on the part of the Board of Ordnance, but gunpowder was a hazardous material and the idea of boiler houses close to production and metal to metal gearing was a large step.

Overall the introduction of steam power could be regarded as the first of two fundamental changes which took place over the manufacturing life of the Mills, the second being the Chemical Revolution - see Chapter Four, both placing considerable demands on the personnel involved.

The Superintendent of the Factory over this period was Lt. Col. W. H. Askwith RA, later General. He was fortunate in having as Assistant Superintendent the very able technical officer Captain F. M. Smith RA, who bore the brunt of the engineering administration. Captain Smith later wrote the influential *Handbook of the Manufacture and Proof of Gunpowder as carried on at the Royal Gunpowder Factory Waltham Abbey.*

Captain Smith was held in high esteem and at his early death a plaque was erected in his memory at Government House.

For completeness of the record, details of the Group A & B Incorporating Mills which were demolished have been included.

1. Group A Incorporating Mills 1857 - 1861 (mill bays demolished)

Group A consisted of a central engine house containing a 30hp beam engine to power the mills, a mechanics shop with power take off from the beam engine, a boiler house and six incorporating mills in bays.

Some general characteristics were initiated, to be followed in the later steam mills Groups C to G - power was transmitted to the mills by an underfloor drive shaft from the engine house; very thick (3ft. in this case) brick mill bay partitions; and outside walls constructed of light material to provide a path of least resistance for any blast away from machinery. The Group A configuration was a series of trapezoidal shaped bays each facing in the opposite direction to the one adjoining.

This configuration was not followed in later mills, possibly partly because the single drive shaft was in retrospect considered to be too long.

In 1861 the mills of Group A were destroyed by an explosion and not rebuilt. However its Engine House, Mechanics Shop and Boiler House survive as Listed Buildings L168 and L176. The shape of the Group A roof gable can still be seen on the end wall of L168. In 1898 a cordite reeling house was built on the Group A site, then in 1908 a cordite press house. After the Second World War, until 1952, this building was used for oxidant preparation and the storage of rocket motor cases and subsequently demolished.

Fig. 37 WAI-0443-04: Aftermath of the Group A explosion in 1861. The roof gable shape is to the right of the chimney.

Fig. 38 WAI-1585-13: Engine House L168, built in 1857. (Photograph 2012)

2. Listed Surviving Elements of Group A Mills

Engine House and Mechanics Shop - L168 Built 1857 (Listed Grade 2*)

The Engine House and Mechanics Shop for the destroyed Group A Incorporating Mills, situated adjacent to the roundabout at the southern end of the Long Walk, still survive. Together with the Boiler House they are the earliest steam related buildings on the site.

The engine was a 30hp compound, supplied by Benjamin Hick & Sons, Soho Ironworks Bolton, powering a single underfloor drive shaft to the mills, with power take off to the Mechanics Shop.

In common with a large proportion of the mills buildings, L168 passed through a variety of uses. Its last working function was, from the mid 1960s, as an experimental 'whisker' factory, where hair like strands of silicon carbide or nitride were produced to reinforce metals to give high strength composite materials for weapons systems.

The Mechanics Shop is the single storey western block of L168. Power for the belt drive was supplied by a second motion shaft from the Engine House. The construction of the shop reflected contemporary application of iron for fireproofing purposes. The roof supported by octagonal cast iron columns with ornate capitals has trusses of round and tee iron with decorative iron compression members. The Mechanics Shop was comprehensively fitted out to provide the most up to date engineering facility. A 4 ton crane, capable of lifting the heaviest edge runners, was mounted on the central pillar.

Particularly impressive was an horizontal boring mill capable of turning the heavy iron mill runners (iron had replaced stone by this time) and incorporating bed plates. An 1869 drawing shows a Lathe House at the end of the Engine House abutting to the Group A mills. A further undated drawing shows "Foundations for Edge Roller Turning Lathe by Smith, Beacock and Tannett, Victoria Foundry (Leeds)".

The new Waltham Abbey mills attracted a considerable amount of interest from the industry home and overseas. Reflecting influence on American practice, in 1858 one of the scions of the American Du Pont family, Lammot Du Pont, visited Waltham Abbey. At that time the Du Pont mills at Hagley on the Brandywine River, near Wilmington, Delaware were the principal producer of black powder in America. Du Pont appears to have been particularly impressed by the Group A Mechanics Shop and also the granulating machine patented by William Congreve's son, also William Congreve - prolific inventor and designer of a military rocket system, who had taken over from his father as Director.

Fig. 39 WAI-0002-01: 2nd William Congreve. (James Lonsdale, National Portrait Gallery)

Fig. 40 WAI-1480-01: Congreve Rocket Troop in Action, 1833.

Within two months of returning to America Du Pont had ordered a similar machine shop to be erected at Hagley with similar equipment.

From their start in gunpowder, reflecting the historic link between gunpowder and explosives and the wider chemical industry, civil and military, the Du Ponts went on to found the great American Du Pont chemical enterprise and the Hagley Yard is now a major museum of gunpowder.

A further major influence on American practice was a treatise on the design and manufacturing processes in the new Waltham Abbey mills written by Major John Baddeley, the Mills Assistant Superintendent, in 1857. This was acknowledged as a vital element in the design and equipping of the central Confederate powder works erected in Augusta Georgia during the American Civil War.

Fig. 41 WAI-0559-01: Lammot du Pont c. 1856. (Hagley Museum Collection)

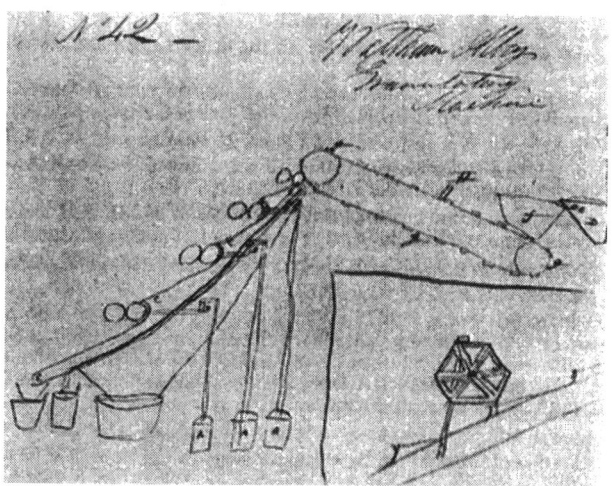

Fig. 42 WAI-0561-01: Drawing by Lammot du Pont of Granulating Machine, 1858. (Eleutherian Mills Historical Library)

Fig. 43 WAI-0563-01: Hagley Mechanics Shop. (The Workers World at Hagley, G. Porter, Hagley Museum, 1981)

Fig. 44 WAI-1581-02: Major J. F. L. Baddeley, Assistant Superintendent Royal Gunpowder Mills. A very able technical officer, author of an influential treatise. (Illustrated London News, Vol. XL, 1862)

Fig. 45 WAI-1548-01: Confederate Powder Works, Augusta, GA, USA, 1863. The designer acknowledged his debt to Maj. Baddeley's treatise and to an adviser who had worked at Waltham Abbey. (Library of Congress)

Fig. 46 WAI-1585-15: L176, built 1857. (Photograph 2012)

Boiler House - L176 Built 1857 (Listed Grade 2*)

This building situated immediately south of the Mechanics Shop is now the café, but in its original incarnation could be regarded as the foundation of a new era since it produced the steam for the first steam mills Group A. In 1902 two new boilers were installed. At the same time a Dynamo House L177 was added to the centre of the east elevation of the Boiler House. It is possible that the boilers were connected to electricity generation. During the time of the site's history as a research establishment the boilers had disappeared and the building was the 'Riggers Shop' and Store.

3. Group B Incorporating Mills 1859 - 1963 (Demolished)

These mills were part of the development of the Lower Island Works, to the south of the Millhead Stream, which commenced in 1801. After years of dereliction they were demolished in 1963 when a link road from the original North Site to the South site was built. In design terms they represented a discontinuity from the Group A mills in that they were water powered instead of steam, with a steam engine only as a reserve in case of water shortage

4. Group C Incorporating Mills - L157 Built 1861 (Listed Grade 1)

Group C was the first of the imposing range of incorporating mills constructed at the eastern edge of the Queens Mead (it is believed so named reflecting its original use as a grazing area for Queen Elizabeth 1's horses - The Queen's Master of Horse lived in Waltham Abbey).

The mill building is T shape comprising a central engine tower, originally housing a steam beam engine with a boiler house at its east end containing two Lancashire boilers. To the north and south of the central tower are two sets of cross bays which held a total of six incorporating mills - three bays on either side. Departing from the trapezoidal arrangement of Group A, the bays were in a line. Each mill located in these bays comprised a pair of vertically mounted cast iron edge runners, weighing about four tons and up to seven feet in diameter, revolving on a circular iron bed. The runners were asymmetric i.e. set at slightly different distances out from the vertical drive shaft to cover a wider track. Runners in earlier mills were stone, some of which can be seen on the site.

Yellow brick laid in English bond was used to construct the engine house, boiler house and partition walls separating the bays. The partition walls are 28inches thick. The outside walls of each bay were of light wood and, rather surprisingly from the safety point of view the roofs were slate.

The possibility of an accident was inescapable. Therefore the design of the light construction front and rear walls was to allow the blast from any accidental explosion to take the line of least resistance to the outside, avoiding transmission of the explosion along the line of adjoining mills. These walls were relatively easy and economic to repair whilst the strong partition walls provided protection and minimised damage to adjoining bays and machinery.

Fig. 47 WAI-1585-10-01: Group C, L157, built 1861. (Photograph 2012)

No detail of the engine has survived. The following is based on general information on what was being supplied at the time by the main supplier to the Mills and the power train which has survived below the mill bays. The engine is believed to have been a twin cylinder compound beam engine of around 30hp (calculated on the mode employed at the time for steam engines). There were two flywheels, one on either side of the engine.

Working pressure in the high pressure cylinder would be about 100psi and the lower about 50psi. The engine would have run at about 18rpm with the edge runners geared down to around 8 rpm. Power transmission from the engine reflected the approach similar to that employed in the textile mills of the time to mitigate the effects of fire - a horizontal drive shaft in an under floor alley. The alleys were lined with cast iron plates bolted together with a top plate forming the mill floor above, as in Group C, or were brick vaulted. A drive shaft ran out from the flywheel on each side of the engine with each shaft driving three sets of runners. The double shaft arrangement gave a better balance and from a production point of view the advantage was that if there were a mishap with one set of runners their shaft could be disconnected and the other set kept running.

Rotative motion of the drive shaft was produced from the reciprocating action of the beam engine via a connecting rod and crank. Drive was engaged or disengaged via a friction clutch consisting of a drum and a 33 teeth pinion wheel. The clutch actuated a 75 teeth bevel wheel which transmitted power to the incorporating bed via a vertical spindle.

For safety reasons the clutch was operated by a remote control rod passing through the drive alley roof to a control wheel in a circular recess on the outside wall on the veranda (see Fig. 54).

The drive shaft was continually spinning. To engage a mill copper edged segments keyed on the shaft were expanded into the drum, transferring motion to the pinion and thus to the bevel wheel and the vertical spindle to the incorporating bed.

Fig. 48 WAI-0101-06: Exterior of steam mills with hand pushed explosives truck on railway running on raised platform. (Strand Magazine, Vol. IX, 1895)

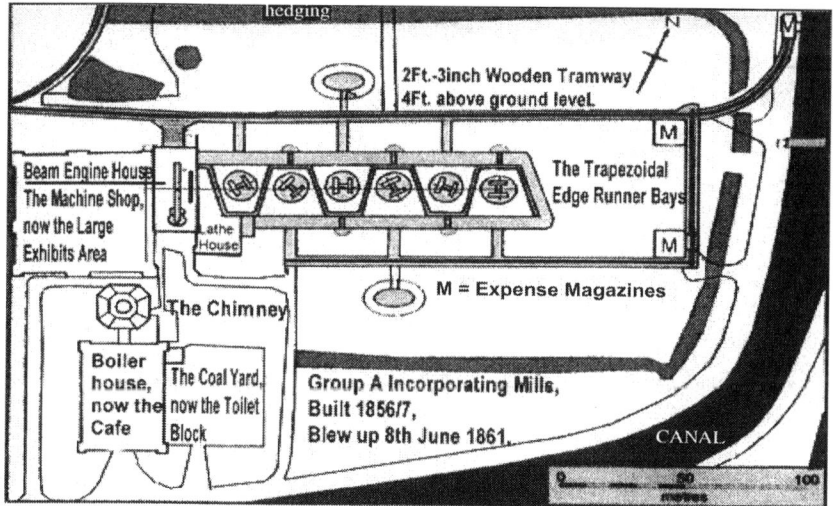

Fig. 49 WAI-0613-01: Group A Configuration, 1857.

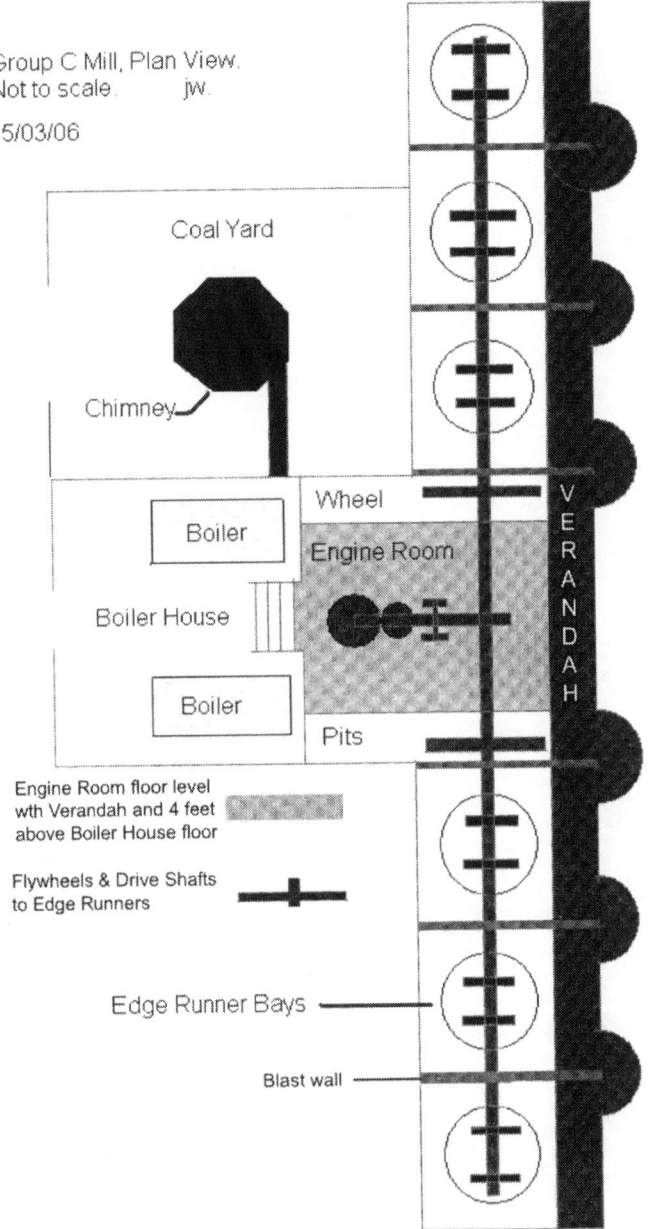

Group C Mill, Plan View.
Not to scale.   jw.

15/03/06

Coal Yard

Chimney

Wheel

Boiler

Engine Room

Boiler House

Boiler

Pits

V E R A N D A H

Engine Room floor level
wth Verandah and 4 feet
above Boiler House floor

Flywheels & Drive Shafts
to Edge Runners

Edge Runner Bays

Blast wall

Fig. 50 WAI-0613-02: Group C Configuration, 1861.

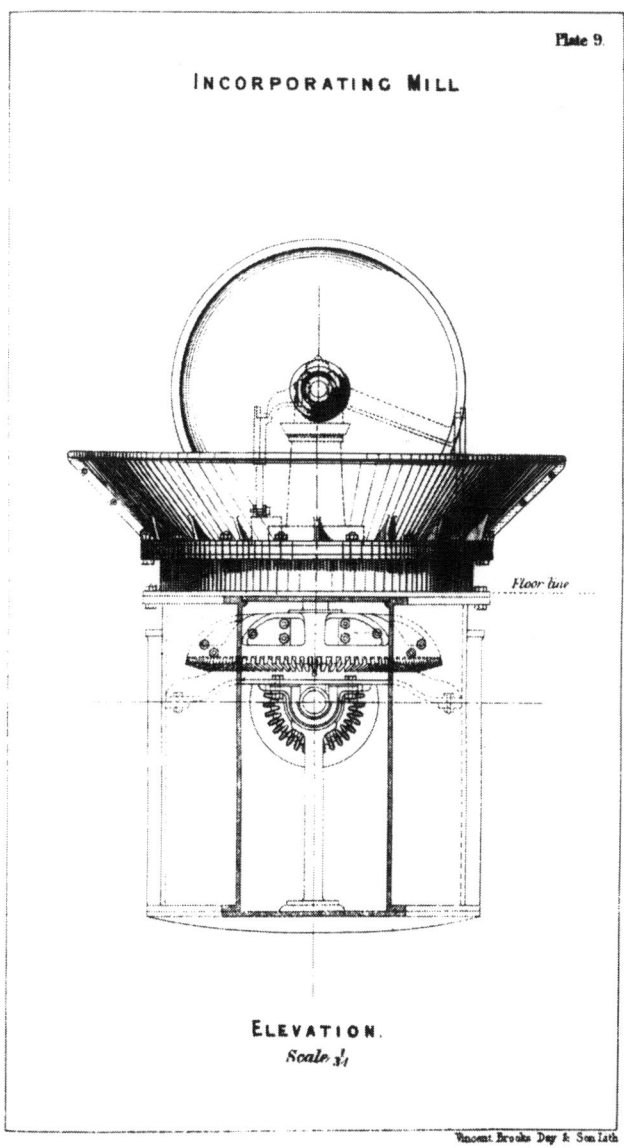

Fig. 51 WAI-0181-09: Incorporating Mill Elevation, showing underfloor drive, incorporating pan and edge runners. (A Handbook of the Manufacture and Proof of Gunpowder as carried on at the Royal Gunpowder Factory Waltham Abbey, Capt. F. M. Smith R A, 1870)

Fig. 52 WAI-1237-02: Incorporating Mill Underfloor Drive Shaft. (Photograph 1993)

Fig. 53 WAI-1584-01: Underfloor Clutch. (Photograph 1993)

The use of underfloor power transmission had two major advantages - it separated two 'alien' systems - metal drive gear and gearing, associated with heat and possible sparks, from the explosive powder dust laden atmosphere of the mill rooms and it removed the risk of a machine part breaking or becoming detached and falling on to the mill bedplate. In addition in the event of an accident the drive machinery was protected and therefore reusable without expensive repair. Great care was exercised in design of the control gear to ensure that the mills could be started without any sudden lurching which would be conducive to explosion.

An important safety feature was the drenching apparatus over each pair of runners. The apparatus comprised of a copper cistern holding 40 gallons of water with a wooden shutter which an explosion would trigger to release the water. This and three other aspects of safety can be seen in one image (Fig. 55) which shows the aftermath of an explosion in Group C - shutter of overturned drenching 'can', worker wearing fireproof clothing - 'lasting', lightweight wall cladding blown out and lighting on external wall avoiding contact with interior.

Architecturally, full advantage was taken of the tall central engine tower to erect a building beyond the strictly utilitarian. It is of Italianate style with a characteristic semi circular ached window to the engine house. The engine and boiler houses had dentil cornices and chamfered brick plinths. In the interior the boiler house had nine trusses with wrought iron tension rods, king rods and decorative cast iron compression members. Overall there is an impression of careful design and construction with the style of the central buildings offsetting the necessarily functional incorporating bays.

Group C was an eminently successful design and became the leading exemplar in the world of the highest level of gunpowder manufacturing practice.

Fig. 54 WAI-0101-08: Remote Starting. (Strand Magazine, Vol. IX, 1895)

Fig. 55 WAI-0009-01: Aftermath of Explosion, 21.10.1890.

5. Groups D, F, G 1867 - 1888

Group D Incorporating Mills L153 Built 1867 (Listed Grade 2*)

Group F Incorporating Mills L145 Built 1878 (Listed Grade 2)

Group G Incorporating Mills L148 Built 1888 (Listed Grade 2*)

Developments in armaments and metals technology led to a steady growth in size of guns and volumes of gunpowder required. In response these further Groups of incorporating mills were built in a line northwards from Group C. commencing six years after Group C and ranging over 20 years.

In an expression of confidence in the Group C design, the design, machinery layout and architecture of Groups D, F and G was basically the same as Group C.

The range of incorporating mills formed one of the most imposing gunpowder structures in Europe.

Fig. 56 WAI-1585-08: Group D, L153, built 1867. (Photograph 2012)

Fig. 57 WAI-1585-05: Group F, L145, built 1878. (Photograph 2012)

Fig. 58 WAI-1585-06: Group G, L148, built 1888.

Fig. 59 WAI-0035 01: Explosion at Group G, L148, 1902.

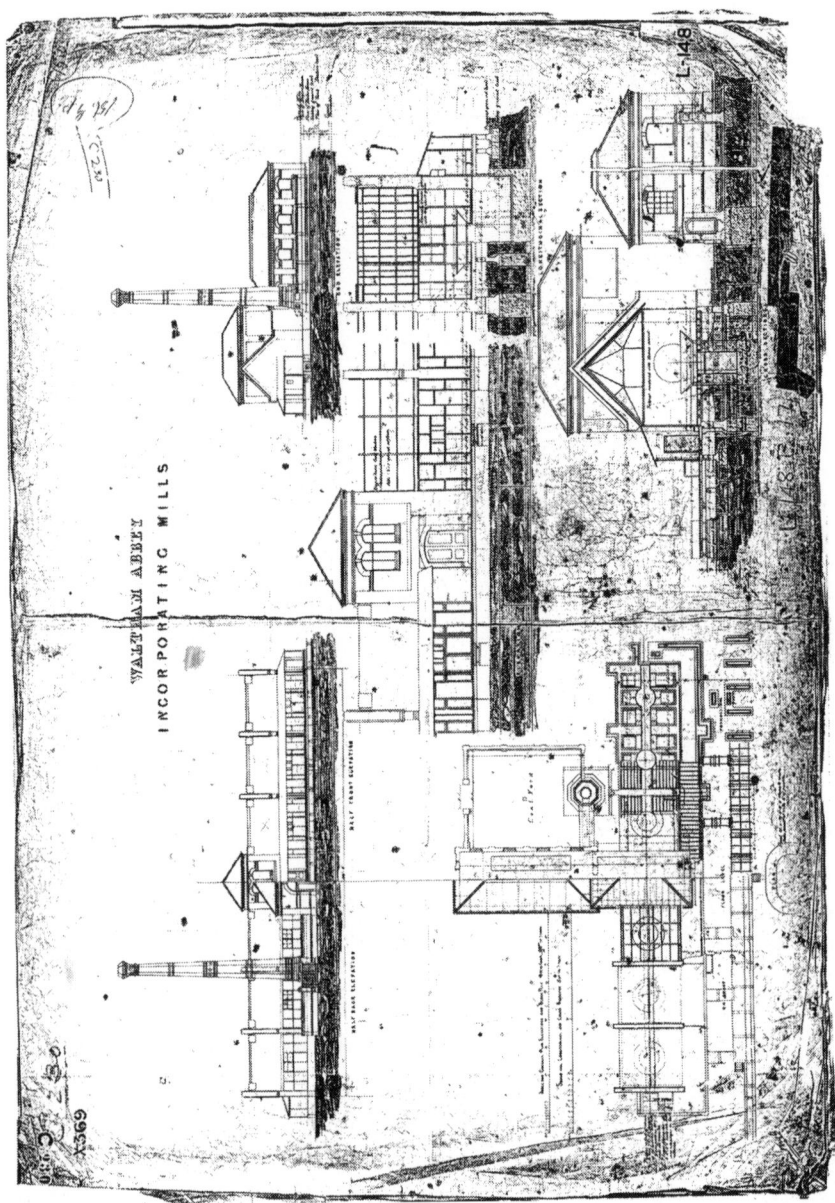

Fig. 60 WAI-1677-01: Group G, L148, built 1888.

6. Group E - L149 Built 1869 (Listed Grade 2*)

Converted to Gunpowder Incorporating Mills 1878

Fig. 61 WAI-1585-07: Group E, L149, built 1869.

Building L149, situated to the east across the Middle Stream from the Queens Mead group, was of particular significance for three reasons:

- It marked the introduction of new forms of powder grain. See below.

- It utilised a form of power - hydraulic from steam driven pumps, which was to become fundamental to the Mills operation over the last part of the 19th century.

- It was converted to gunpowder incorporation from its original function.

See further commentary on hydraulic power at Waltham Abbey in the Chapter: The Cordite Era and the Rise of Chemical Science.

New Guns, New Powders - Pellet, Pebble, Prismatic, Brown

Pellet - 1861

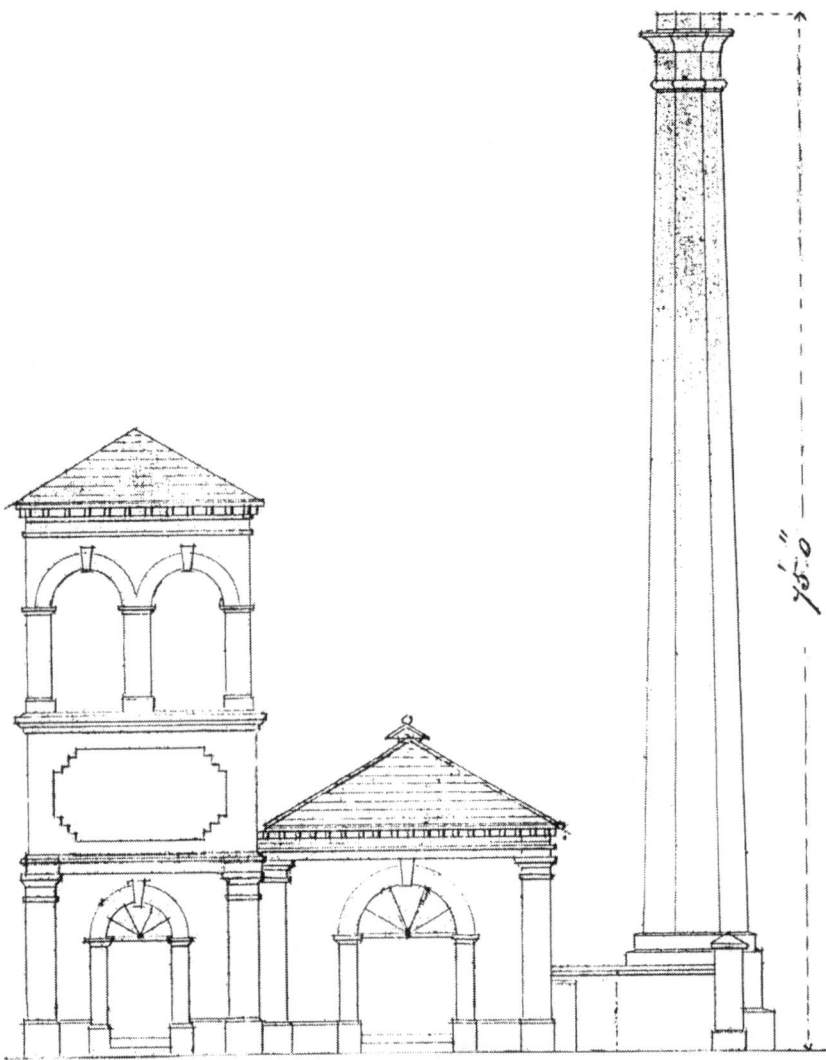

Fig. 62 WAI-1690-01: Pellet Powder Buildings, built 1869, later designation L149.

With older shorter barrel guns the powder had to burn quickly to give the projectile the necessary velocity within the short space of time it was in the barrel. New larger guns being introduced required larger charges. However the force of powder in larger quantity brought with it the possibility of damage to the gun. The Governmental Special Committee on Gunpowder decided in response that powder with grains of cylindrical shape and larger size - termed 'Pellet', made from hydraulically powered moulding (pressing / shaping) dusted grain, should be produced and after a lengthy delay, possibly caused by lack of funds, in 1869 manufacture commenced with the building of L149. Powder burned from the outer surface inwards and therefore in a larger grain took longer to burn to the centre. This, in conjunction with the more regular grain shape, produced a slower burning rate, rate of combustion, together with a steadier pressure on the projectile and therefore lessened the possibility of gun damage.

In the meantime the Committee had been restructured as the Committee on Gunpowder and Explosives and their deliberations resulted in the adoption of pebble powder for larger guns.

Pebble - Ca. 1871

Investigation into a grain suitable for larger guns continued. Around 1871 a cube shaped larger grain, made by cutting press cake was introduced - termed 'Pebble'.

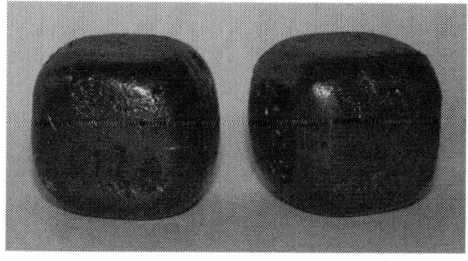

Fig. 63 WAI-0591-01: Plaster model of Pebble Powder.

Prismatic - 1881

Neither Pellet nor Pebble was entirely satisfactory. Whilst slower burning was being achieved the burning surface declined as the projectile moved along the barrel and velocity therefore lessened. In Pebble the maximum charge that could be used to increase velocity was limited by the production of high pressure waves, potentially damaging to the powder chamber. Merely increasing grain size as gun size increased could not be continued indefinitely. In response In 1881 a further large shape variant was introduced - hexagonal, termed 'Prismatic' powder, made by hydraulically powered moulding of dusted grain. Crucially as well as a new shape the grains were perforated. This meant that whilst burning at the outer surfaces lowered their area burning at the inner surfaces increased theirs. Perforations could be designed to provide an initial, inner surface area that was equal to or greater than the outer. Thus it was possible with careful manufacture to produce the 'progressive burning' which was required for guns - i.e. as the gases expanded the momentum of the projectile rose steadily as it moved up the barrel producing maximum velocity as it left the barrel.

Fig. 64 WAI-0590-01: Plaster model of Prismatic Powder.

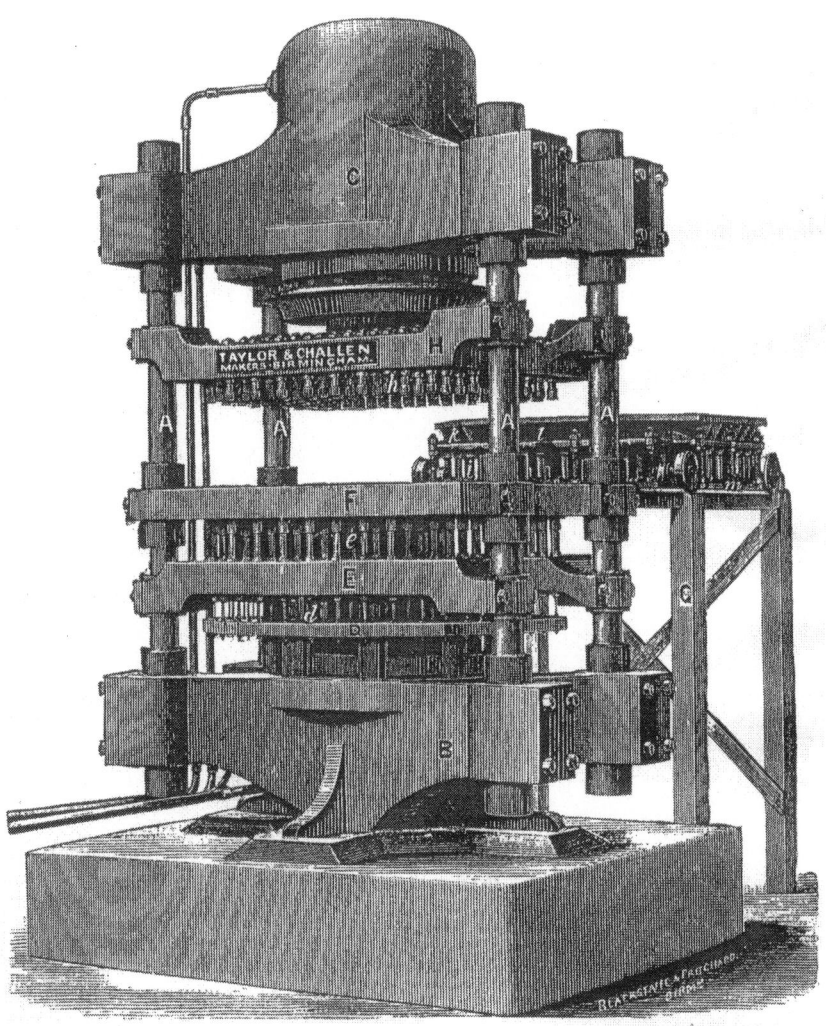

Fig. 65 WAI-1677-01: Prismatic Moulding Machine (as seen in Fig. 66) constructed for the Royal Gunpowder Mills by Taylor & Challen,, Birmingham. (The Manufacture of Explosives, O. Guttmann, 1895)

Fig. 66 WAI-0457-11: The Prismatic Moulding Room. (Strand Magazine, Vol. IX, 1895)

Brown

Prism powders were regarded as having the most successful ballistic performance for larger guns. Their quality was further enhanced by the use of charcoal in their manufacture made from rye straw. Reflecting the colour produced, these powders, which also had good smokeless quality, were termed 'Brown' or 'Cocoa'. Prismatic cocoa powders represented the peak of gunpowder as a military propellant.

New Powders, New Power source - The Rise of Hydraulics

L149 initiates the steam powered hydraulic system at Waltham Abbey

The manufacture of pellet powder from grain required high pressure and the capability to form a regular shape. Fortunately at this time William Armstrong, the Newcastle shipbuilder and arms systems manufacturer, had developed, arising from his lifelong interest in water power, a system of hydraulic power based on steam driven pumps and accumulator towers. This was ideal for gunpowder manufacture and the Mills quickly adopted the idea.

L149 therefore comprised, as well as a boiler house serving a steam engine in an engine house, a central hydraulic accumulator tower. Thus although it externally appeared to be of the same configuration as the rest of the incorporating mills, i.e. with a central tower housing a beam engine, in fact in this case it housed hydraulic machinery and the engine house was on a lower level.

Moulding

Pellet powders were made by hydraulically compressing in metal blocks and the process carried on in L149 was termed 'moulding'. Investigation continued into the type of powder most suitable for larger charges and it was later decided to concentrate on an alternative - Pebble powders. These were cut directly from pressed material and therefore did not require moulding. Accordingly in 1878 L149 was converted to a gunpowder incorporating mill with what had become the standard six cross bays, designated Incorporating Mill Group E. The date plaque on the front of the accumulator tower therefore refers to the date when the mills conversion took place and not the original building date.

At first sight the reversal of policy on powder type would appear to have left the hydraulic equipment redundant. However it is likely that it was employed in Guncotton pressing and the advent of prismatic powders brought a further moulding requirement.

It is not clear whether the rotary drive shaft engine required for gunpowder incorporation was also employed to power the hydraulic pumps or whether another engine was employed. However, it can be deduced from the engine house height that it could not have accommodated a beam engine and it was therefore of horizontal type.

In terms of the classic changes of the Industrial Revolution - the move from water power to steam and from wood to iron - the Waltham Abbey Mills were relatively late in the day. However, after an initial false start the steam mills which followed were a notable design success and set an international standard of excellence in the manufacture of gunpowder.

The Listed Incorporating Mills - The Cordite Era and the Rise of Chemical Science: 1898 - 1943

"I myself was soon so hotly engaged, loading and firing away enveloped in the smoke I created, and the cloud which hung about me from the continued fire of my comrades, that I could see nothing for a few minutes but the red flash of my own piece amongst the white vapour clinging to my very clothes. This has often seemed to me the greatest drawback upon our present system of fighting."

(Recollections of Rifleman Harris, 1827)

Smokeless Powders

In the late 1880s outwardly it must have appeared to many that gunpowder had successfully met the challenges of the larger guns. But there was a continual pressure for advance in military technology including propellant, particularly an effective 'smokeless powder'. Attention turned increasingly to the scientist and specifically to the new science of organic chemistry.

Frederick, later Sir Frederick, Abel, the first Chemical Advisor to the War Department, after extensive experimentation and development at the Government Laboratory at Woolwich and at Waltham Abbey, had successfully developed the chemically based Guncotton (Nitrocellulose), patented in 1865. It was a highly effective military demolition agent and explosive filling for mines and torpedoes. But this very explosive effectiveness militated against its use as a propellant. The nitrocottons were fibrous in form and in the confined combustion of the gun breech the hot gases formed were forced into the pores of the material, producing an excessive rate of burning and an uneven and excessive pressure on the gun leading to damage.

In 1886 the Frenchman Vielle achieved the first chemically based smokeless powder suitable for use as a propellant - Poudre B. This dealt with the problem of porosity by gelatinising the nitrocotton - less highly nitrated collodion cotton of lower nitrogen content, with the solvent ether alcohol. The advantages of the new material went far beyond less smoke. It had about three times the power of gunpowder, producing greater pressure in a smaller space, enabling a smaller cartridge, a smaller bullet and correspondingly a smaller calibre rifle., which meant that a soldier in this case the French Army could carry a significantly greater number of cartridges and fire from a greater range than any other army in Europe.

Not surprisingly in an era of intense Great Power rivalry the discovery led to a flurry of intensive activity amongst other researchers. After extensive experimentation and trial, often attended by the risk of accidental explosion, much to the astonishment of the scientific establishment it was discovered in 1887 by the Swedish inventor Alfred Nobel that the power of guncotton could be moderated by gelatinising it with another powerful chemical explosive, Nitroglycerine, producing a smokeless powder termed 'Ballistite'.

In Britain the concept was developed by Messrs. Abel, Dewar and Dupre into an extruded, i.e. pressed through dies, material which they termed 'Cordite' after the strands or cords which were extruded, patented in 1889.

Fig. 67 WAI-1522-01: Frederick Abel's Chemical Laboratory at Woolwich (built 1864).

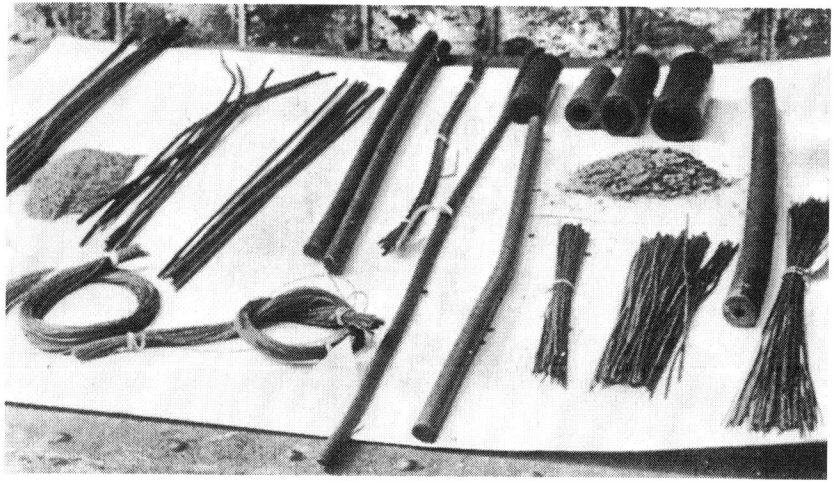

Fig. 68 WAI-0102-08: Sticks of tubular and solid cordite. (The Navy and Army Illustrated, 14.10.1899)

In a very short space of time the 600 year evolution of gunpowder as the world explosive, civil and military, was ended by a revolution in chemical science and cordite had become the propellant of the British Forces.

The age of chemical science had begun.

The Move to Cordite

At Waltham Abbey the entire structure and operation had to be adapted to the new technology.

After an initial concentration on the South Site the focus of cordite manufacture shifted to the North Site, with drying remaining on the South Site. In 1897 a nitroglycerine plant was built at Edmonsey on the North Site and over the last years of the 19th century buildings were adapted and new processing facilities built on the North Site, ultimately being termed the Cordite Factory or as the locals said 'The Cordite'.

Fig. 69 WAI-0182-01: The first group of workers to carry out cordite manufacture at Waltham Abbey, 1891.

The listed gunpowder incorporating mills were totally converted to cordite production.

Conversion involved the removal of the gunpowder edge runners, covering over of the underfloor transmission train and installation of cordite incorporators or in the case of two mills pressing machinery. The power source remained the beam engines, but this time driving overhead line shafts with belt drive running to each incorporator. Around 1905 when the Mills began to generate its own electricity from the Power House the beam engines were finally replaced by 30v dc electric motors.

Fortunately for industrial archaeology, the method employed to remove the edge runners - simply cutting the vertical drive shaft to the runners and letting the gearing drop down into the drive tunnel, meant that this, together with the undisturbed main drive shaft, can still be seen.

Fig. 70 WAI-1237-01: Gearing in Driveshaft Tunnel.

The Manufacture of Cordite

Although obviously the materials, machinery etc. were very different, In very broad overview terms the cordite manufacturing process was akin to gunpowder with batches of material passing through a sequence of operations to produce the final product and gunpowder processing terms were continued into Cordite.

1. Guncotton - produced in Guncotton factory on South Site by nitration of cotton. Transported in moist state to magazine on North Site.

2. Guncotton Drying - taken from magazine as required and dried in Stoves.

3. Nitroglycerine - produced by nitration of glycerine in Nitroglycerine plant.

4. Mixing - Dry Guncotton and Nitroglycerine blended in Mixing House into 'Paste'.

5. Incorporation - Paste transported to Incorporating Mill and incorporated (combined) with Acetone solvent, to promote gelatinisation of Guncotton / combination and create plastic consistency required for pressing. Mineral jelly (Vaseline) added to promote stability in storage producing 'Dough'.

6. Pressing - Dough is pressed (extruded) through dies into cord (stick) shape.

Small diameters for rifle or pistol use are pressed separately in Rifle Presses.

7. Cutting - Large diameter cords cut into manageable lengths.

8. Reeling - Small diameter cord is wound on to reels.

9. Stove Drying - cords are dried in steam Stoves - Tray Stoves or Reel Drying Houses, to drive off Acetone vapour - which is recovered in Acetone Recovery Plant.

10. Acetone Recovery - acetone vapour conveyed by pipe to Acetone Recovery plant.

11. Blending to produce uniform ballistic results

Small diameter blending - In Reeling House strands from ten dried reels of small diameter are wound together to form one string on a separate reel. Six of these reels are wound together to form one rope, which therefore consists of sixty small diameter filaments which are cut into lengths and form the filling of rifle and pistol cartridges.

Large diameter blending - Large diameters blended by hand.

12. Packing - Cords are packed into boxes.

The listed gunpowder incorporating mills which performed updated cordite functions were:

Incorporation and Pressing		
Mills	**Gunpowder**	**Cordite**
L145 Group F	Incorporating	Incorporating
L148 Group G	Incorporating	Incorporating
L149 Group E	Incorporating	Incorporating
L153 Group D	Incorporating	Pressing (extruding)
L157 Group C	Incorporating	Pressing (extruding)

Other cordite converted or new builds are detailed in the following chapters.

The cordite produced was an outstanding success - robust, reliable and capable of an infinite range of variations to suit different requirements. For over 50 years it remained the main British Forces propellant, into the 1950s.

Having introduced a major change in power technology in the mid 19th century, at the end of the century the Mills, over a very short space of time, managed a total change in the nature and technology of the propellant, from a basis of natural ingredients - saltpetre, charcoal and sulphur - for gunpowder, to the chemical base nitroglycerine and nitrocellulose for cordite, with all the implications this carried - a new, unfamiliar plant, conversion of old plant and buildings, new manufacturing, new materials handling, revised safety procedures, training of staff, new laboratory and testing procedures, etc. - an impressive achievement.

Fig. 71 WAI-1591-07: Guncotton Drying Stove Racks for trays of guncotton, with drying pipe. Racks were contained in timber round houses surrounded by brick revetments set in earth mounds. Warm drying air was fed in by pipe from a central engine house blowing air over a heat exchanger.

Fig. 72 WAI-0443-10: Edmonsey Nitroglycerine Nitrating Hill, 1917. The manufacturing process relied on gravity flow between processing units. The lift, later replaced by a compressed air system, took glycerine and acids to the Charge House at the peak of the hill, from where the process commenced. (The Navy and Army Illustrated, 14.10.1899)

Fig. 73 WAI-1525-01: Mixing House Interior. The walls were zinc lined to prevent build up of hazardous dry guncotton dust; the floor was lead lined. Nitroglycerine was run into a lead burette and poured on to dry guncotton in a bag beneath the burette (right of image). The resultant 'paste' was taken to the mixing table (left of image) hand kneaded by operative, pushed through a phosphor bronze sieve and bagged.

Fig. 74 WAI-0443-26: Cordite Incorporating Machinery, 1917.

Fig. 75 WAI-0102-20: Cordite Press.

Fig. 76 WAI-0443-28: Vertical Cordite Press, shielded by safety mantle, 1917.

Fig. 77 WAI-0443-27: Rifle Presses for Small Diameter Cords, 1917.

Fig. 78 WAI-1524-01: Hand cutting lengths of larger diameter cordite.

Fig. 79 WAI-0247-02: Winding smaller diameters of cordite onto reels. (Sixty Years a Queen, 1897)

Fig. 80 WAI-0443-31: Trays of larger diameter cordite en route from North Site to South Site Drying Stoves, 1917.

Fig. 81 WAI-1657-01: Aerial View of the South Site Cobb Mead Cordite Drying Stoves of 1902 - 4. (NMR 4825/43)

Fig. 82 WAI-0102-22: Drying Reels of Cordite. (The Navy and Army Illustrated, 14.10.1899)

Fig. 83 WAI-0443-54: Model of Acetone Recovery Plant.

Fig. 84 WAI-0101-22: 'Ten Stranding' of Cordite. (Strand Magazine, Vol. IX, 1895)

Fig. 85 WAI-0102-21: Blending 60 strands of cordite into one 'rope'. (The Navy and Army Illustrated, 14.10.1899)

Fig. 86 WAI-1587-01: Hand blending larger diameters of cordite and packing them into boxes.

Fig .87 WAI-0346-01: (next page) Cordite Workers and Management of No.2 Press House, 1917. In uniform, centre - Lt. Col. Evans, Superintendent of the Factory (replacing Col. Fisher). On his left - Lt. E. L. Blee, Danger Buildings Officer, after service on the Western Front (20 years later in WW2 Lt. Blee was recalled to the Colours to do the same job). On Lt. Col. Evans right, Lady Superintendent. Next to Lt. Blee - Mr. J. M.Thomson, Factory Manager. Next to Mr. Thomson - Mr. P. G. Knapman, last Superintendent of the Factory.

The Listed Incorporating Mills - The Research Era: 1945 - 1991

"Organic chemistry just now is enough to drive one mad. It gives me the impression of a primeval forest full of the most remarkable things, a monstrous and boundless thicket, with no way of escape, into which one may well dread to enter."

(Friedrich Wohler, 1835)

Fig. 88 WAI-0487-01: Demolition of No.3 Incorporating Mill, September 1936.

The Millhead and WW2

The advent of the gleaming new steam mills on Queens Mead did not spell the end of the venerable water driven mills on the Millhead. Inevitably they moved into a period of lower production, but gradually established a niche as a supplier of Service fuze powders with the charcoal content based on dogwood, to the point where they became the sole supplier of Service fuze powders.

By 1937 four Millhead incorporating mills were still working, with nos. 2 and 3 demolished and the others derelict. With rising demand important improvements were made in charcoal production - burning in rotary carbonising plant instead of the cylinders which had been introduced at the beginning of the 19th. century, grinding in separate disintegrators instead of gunpowder mills, mechanical sieving replacing laborious hand sieving.

After the building of new Ordnance factories in the late 1930s the Millhead then supplied millcake from the incorporating mills to these factories where it was worked up into finished fuze powders.

The Millhead connection with fuze powder extended within the factory. It supplied the South Site RD202 AA fuze production unit with dogwood charcoal. RD202 was a gunpowder type product comprising charcoal fuel, ammonium perchlorate oxidiser and starch as a binder.

WW2 and Closure

It had become obvious in the 1930s that the Mills location was very vulnerable to air attack from Europe and a programme was instituted to move centres of explosive production generally to safer areas in the west. However when war broke out in 1939 the process had not been completed and once again Waltham Abbey was called on to significantly increase output of guncotton and propellant and also the vital high explosive RDX. The original intention of the RDX plant was to act as a test pilot plant for a new factory to the west of the country. However by the outbreak of war planning had not been completed and the Mills found itself catapulted into the role of the sole producer of RDX, until 1941, when the Royal Ordnance Factory at Bridgwater in Somerset was opened.

RDX and Guncotton were produced on the South Site. Other principal products, Cordite and Tetryl on the North Site

The End of the Old Millhead Stream Mills, 15 November 1940 - Number 4 Incorporating Mill

By 1940 the last gunpowder producing mill on the Millhead Stream was Building 191 No. 4 Incorporating Mill situated by the bridge on the road from the roundabout to the main gates just to the east of H7 Reel Drying House.

On the night of 15th November 1940 a Luftwaffe pilot released a parachute mine above Waltham Abbey and it drifted slowly down. Whether this was specifically intended to land on the Mills is not known. They certainly knew the function of the site - cordite production, as described in the previous chapter - but parachute mines drift with the wind so are unsuited to precision bombing. Fate decreed that of all places it should land close by the last venerable mill on the Millstream, destroying the Reel Store associated with H7 Reel Drying House and the timber structure of Mill No.4 but not the machinery.

As the mill machinery had survived it could have resumed production of fuze powder millcake. However by this time the new factories were capable of undertaking the full production process and it was decided to terminate production on the Millhead.

Fig. 89 WAI-0443-68: Damage to No.4 Incorporating Mill, 15.11.1940.

Thus an unknown German pilot, in a victory of a kind, unwittingly brought to an end military gunpowder production for the Crown at Waltham Abbey. From its deceptively leafy surroundings the Millhead Stream and its mills for over 200 years had in conditions of secrecy seen its product employed in the defence history of the nation from the smallest skirmish to set piece battles in land, sea and air, the protection of trade routes, the cataclysmic events of the formation of Empire and its protection and two Great Wars of national salvation. Now they slipped back into history as quietly and unobtrusively as they had worked.

There was however one final twist to the Millhead story. Phoenix like, No. 10 incorporating mill was dismantled, reconditioned and re-erected at the Chorley Royal Ordnance Factory where again presumably it was employed in the production of fuze powders.

Fig. 90 WAI-0119-01: Ruins of the Last Pair of Mills in the 1950s.

CLOSING OF R.G.P.F., WALTHAM ABBEY   S.S.5/531

1.   The Royal Gunpowder Factory, Waltham Abbey will cease to be operated on munitions production on Saturday 28th July next, after which date the premises and plant will be utilised by this Ministry as an Experimental Station, estimated provisionally to provide employment for about 250 workpeople.   The present labour strength will therefore fall to be reduced to approximately 400 200.
2.   In accordance with the procedure laid down in Memos. No. S.S.5/275 and S.S.5/438 the Managing Chemist is requested in consultation with C.S.A.R.D. and the Regional Controller, M.O.S., to arrange with the regional officers of the Ministry of Labour & National Service for the retention of a balanced labour force of 250 and the release of all other industrial workers by 28th July, 1945.

Ministry of Supply internal Memo 1945

Fig. 91 WAI-0596-01: Ministry of Supply memorandum recording the closure of the Royal Gunpowder Factory, Waltham Abbey, on Saturday 28th July 1945.

Closure of the Royal Gunpowder Mills as a Production Factory and Re-Opening as a Research Centre

By 1943 new Ordnance Factory building had progressed to the extent that Waltham Abbey could cease manufacture, apart from Tetryl, which continued until the next year 1944.

Over 200 years of Governmental gunpowder and later chemical explosive production came officially to an end when the Factory was closed on 28th July 1945. The Mills had operated in conditions of secrecy and their end was similarly muted.

But the life of the site was by no means over - two short days later on 30th July 1945 it opened as the Experimental Station of the Armament Research Department.

From the 18th century official research into explosives had been centred on the Royal Laboratory at Woolwich, ultimately becoming the Armament Research Department. At the end of the Second World War it was decided that explosives experimental work should be concentrated in a dedicated centre and the site at Waltham Abbey was chosen.

In November 1944, five months after D-Day, a senior civil servant, writing from Fort Halstead, had described the unsatisfactory situation of the Armament Research Department at Woolwich, which had suffered from bomb damage and was generally in poor condition and submitted a proposal that a fundamental explosives research and manufacturing research group should be established at Waltham Abbey.

Dr. G. Rotter, Director of Research at the Armament Research Department, commented as follows:

"Generally speaking, I think it is a very good report and the scheme finally proposed an excellent one."

"Waltham Abbey has tradition. It is well situated and would provide most of the facilities required for manufacture on both experimental and full scale working as well as for storage. I think that certain of the buildings would also make excellent laboratories."

"Transfer of the whole of the propellant work to Waltham Abbey would also have important advantages. An enormous saving in cost would result as compared with a completely new site."

The Research Era 1945 - 1991

A year after the move, in 1946 with the transfer of further explosives and propellant scientific staff from Woolwich, the Chemical Research Department was created, in 1947 changing to Chemical Research and Development Establishment, in 1948 to Explosives Research and Development Establishment - ERDE, this title remaining until 1977 when reflecting the direction of activity it changed to Propellants, Explosives and Rocket Motor Establishment - PERME and finally in 1984 the Royal Armament Research and Development Establishment - RARDE. Following various Governmental science re organisations, the work of RARDE was transferred to other locations and the site finally closed in 1991.

Following the move from Woolwich an extensive programme of building refurbishment was undertaken:

- The concrete blast walls - 'traverses' and railway lines alongside the incorporating mills were removed, partly by

German prisoner of war labour and the buildings gradually converted to laboratories.

- The railway ran along an open raised veranda. The height was necessary due to the flooding which affected the site. When the conversion to laboratories took place the veranda was glassed in to allow weather protected movement along the range of mills.

The buildings had been used for the manufacture of the new plastic propellant and filling into rocket motors. This was gradually moved to the South Site.

The Victorian builders had built well, with a high standard of workmanship. Little structural work was needed for conversion, the majority of work concentrated on interior refurbishment and equipment installation. The Mills configuration with individual bays proved eminently suitable for installation of laboratories and small scale processing. Thus what could have been an abandoned Victorian relic became instead an establishment which was to play a leading part in Britain's advance into high-tech defence in the second half of the 20th century.

Whether and how to preserve the buildings of Britain's industrial past is now a subject of national interest, the solution now often being found in converting them to commercial or cultural use. The Mills conversion was one of the earliest, and successful, examples of what has come to be known as adaptive re-use of industrial buildings long before the concept came to the fore.

The work of the Establishment covered research, development and advice on all Service non nuclear explosives and propellants, including rocket propellant, from the fundamental organic chemistry through to pilot scale production and later expanded into non metallic materials with a Service application.

Fig. 92 WAI-0370-03: Line of Mills with Blast Wall / Traverse.

Fig. 93 WAI-0405-01: Demolition of Traverse 1945.

105

Fig. 94 WAI-1035-01: Mills converted to laboratories with glazed raised platform.

This extended to include manufacture of a diffuse range of specialised rubber and plastic defence related components, such as seals for gun mounts and radomes for fighter aircraft, and high strength composites. The Establishment also manufactured a range of specialised propellants such as the ejector material for aircraft ejector seats.

Broadly, research activity on the two sites of the Establishment split into:

North Site - the present heritage centre, including the listed buildings:

- Explosives
- Materials including polymer R & D
- Analysis and Ingredients

Propellant research was initially undertaken on the North Site and later moved to the South Site. Materials was later reorganised with sections going to other branches.

South Site - now occupied by a country park, housing and a distribution centre:

- Solid Propellant research and production - gun, rocket; military and civil
- Design and production of specialised propellants, defence components and military equipment
- Development of high strength composite materials

The scope and emphasis of research was an ongoing process reflecting developments in the defence world in conjunction with initiatives from the Establishment and Governmental budgetary policy. Inevitably some research topics reached the end of their life and others took their place and use of the buildings reflected this. The following is an overview of the research activity in the listed buildings on the North Site, i.e.the present heritage area, at a point in time. For the sake of completeness of the historical record non listed buildings are also included.

Fig. 95 WAI-0039-01: Factory Staff Prior to Closure.

Explosives

Incorporating Mill Group G - L148 - Listed

Refinement of existing explosive formulations and development of new compositions. Research on and development of sensitive initiating explosives including development up to pilot scale of safe manufacturing processes for initiators.

Incorporating Mill Group E - L149 - Listed

Safety of explosives - Safety advice to users of Safety and Hazard tests. Issue of safety certificates.

Study of the risk of accidental ignition involving research into impact, shock, friction. fragment attack and electrostatic hazard.

Detonation - studies of release of energy from explosives, including:

- Assessment of underwater explosives (at Newtons Pool)
- Noise evaluation, e.g. simulation of Concorde sonic boom
- Remotely controlled handling of hazardous materials
- Time resolved spectroscopy of transient events
- High speed photography

Fig. 96 WAI-0421-01: Rotter Impact Machine. Standard safety test for explosives. Devised by Dr. G. Rotter.

Fig. 97 WAI-0192-33: Underwater Testing at Newtons Pool, 1977. Explosion at maximum plume height.

Fig. 98 WAI-0413-09: Remote preparation of sensitive material using master - slave unit.

Fig. 99 WAI-0394-01: North Site Firing Point 2. Beckman & Whitley 339B streak high speed camera for explosion detonations, 1970s.

Non - Metallic Materials Research, Polymer Research and Development

L134 - Non Listed
L137 - Non Listed
L143 - Non Listed

Polymer chemistry and physics, research into characteristics of polymeric plastic materials and their reaction to hostile environments.

Study of plastics and rubbers and development and applications - Serial production of components in these materials including Dracones for fuel storage, flexible fuel tanks, conducting rubber for armoured fighting vehicle tracks, nylon driving bands and obturating rings for shells.

Investigation of ethyl cellulose inhibition for EDB rocket motors. Polymer synthesis with possible application as rocket motor binders.

Fig. 100 WAI-1226-01: Tensometer testing the breaking point of plastics, 1968.

Fig. 101 WAI-0394-06: Servotest Machine. Dynamic mechanical fatigue testing of materials, 1970s.

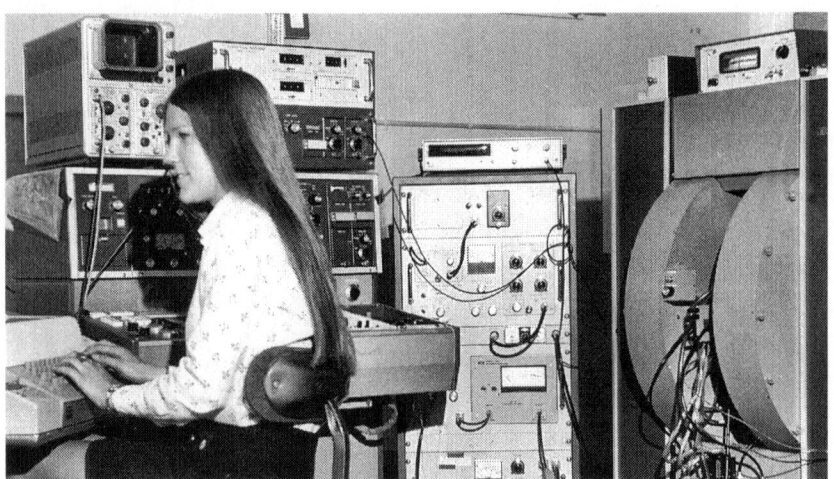

Fig. 102 WAI-0394-05: NMR Spectrometer. Chemical analysis of polymers, 1970s.

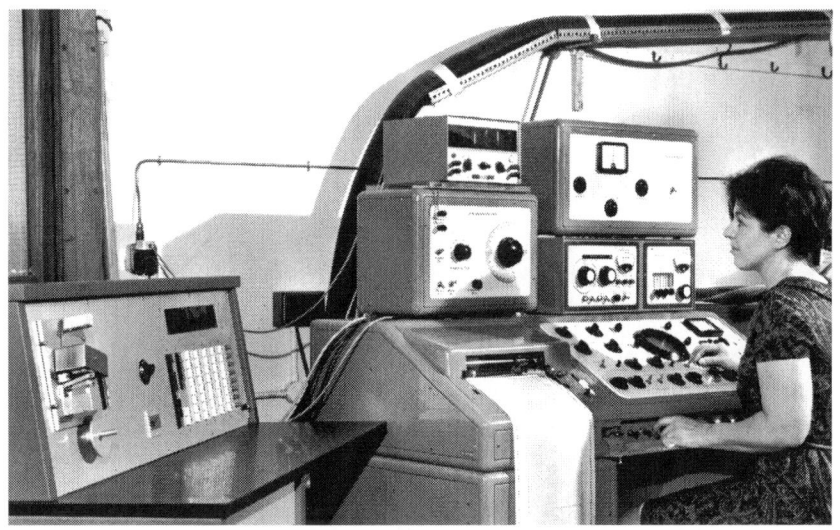

Fig. 103 WAI-0270-23: Nuclear Magnetic Resonance Spectroscopy, 1968.

Incorporating Mill Group G - L148 - Listed

Adhesion - Mechanical properties of adhesives and rocket propellants including adhesive strength measurement in relation to its effect on sealant efficiency.

Rheology of Rocket Propellants - Rheology is the science of deformation and flow of matter.

'Whiskers'

Incorporating Mill Group C - L157 - Listed

Research into strengthening of thermoplastics by filling with fibres: asbestos, glass, carbon and applications of strengthened materials e.g. Kevlar body armour. Strengthening of metals by ceramic 'whiskers'.

Fig. 104 WAI-1234-01: Rheogoniometer - measuring angles of the faces of crystals.

L168 - previously Engine House and Mechanics Shop - Listed

Development of manufacturing method and production of silicon carbide or nitride whiskers.

Fig.105 WAI-0486-02: 'Bran Tub' furnaces for synthesis of silicon nitride whiskers, 1968. Located on the second level of the "Tower" in L168.

Fig. 106 WAI-0270-04: Removing Silicon Nitride Whiskers, 1968.

Analysis and Ingredients (General Chemistry)

L155 - Non Listed

- Explosives and synthetic chemistry.
- Investigation of physical and chemical properties and reactions of explosives and ingredients of propellants and polymers, e.g. curing agents, stabilisers, antioxidants.
- Characterisation, employing chromatography, spectroscopy and microscopy.
- Studies to optimise yield and purity.

L153 - Non Listed

- Gas Kinetics.
- Research into gas phase reactions.

Fig. 107 WAI-0486-03: Gas Handling Line.

Analysis - Compatibility and Stability

Ensuring stability of explosives in service use and their compatibility with other materials

Incorporating Mill Group F - L145 - Listed

- Thin layer and gas chromatography.
- Atomic absorption spectrophotometry.
- Polymer fractionation.
- Instrumental analysis - spectroscopy: infra-red, ultra-violet.
- Nuclear magnetic resonance.
- X-ray crystallography.

Fig. 108 WAI-0140-12: Gas Chromatography, 1968.

Fig. 109 WAI-0394-11: Mass Spectrometer linked to Gas Chromatograph, 1970s.

Fig. 110 WAI-0192-18: Solid Propellant Gas Analysis, 1977.

121

L146 - Non Listed

X-ray crystallography

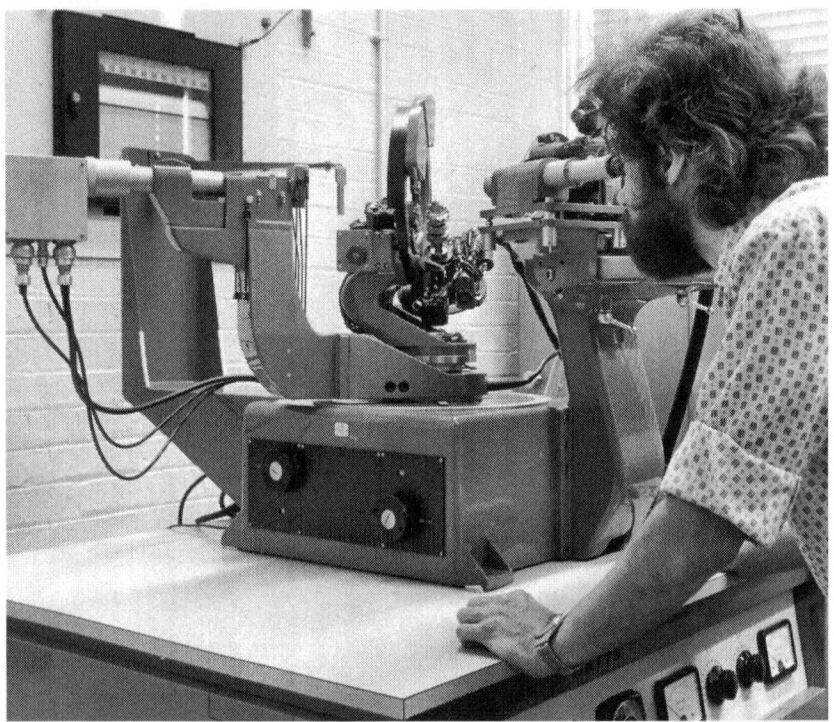

Fig. 111 WAI-1133-02: X-ray Crystallography - the study of the crystal structure of explosives, 1970s.

L119 - Non Listed

Elemental microanalysis.

H10 - Non Listed

Mathematics and Computing.

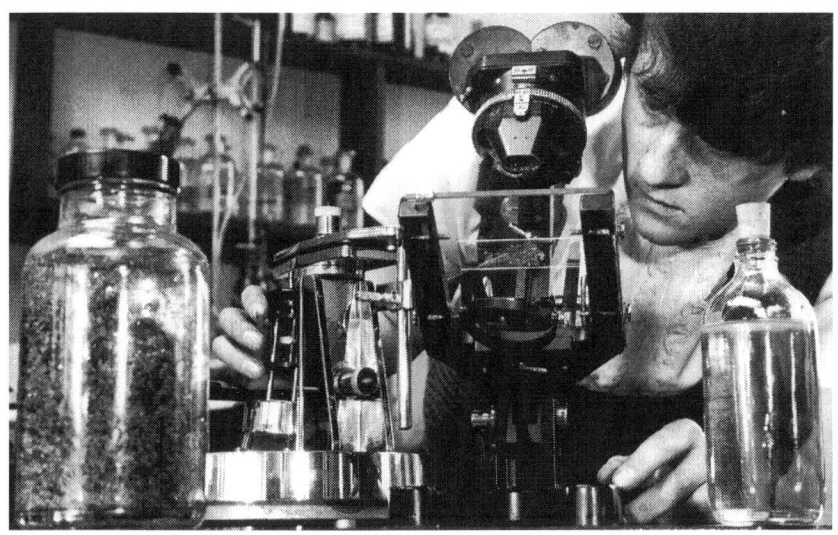

Fig. 112 WAI-0270-38: Use of Micro Manipulator in Examination of Crystals, 1968.

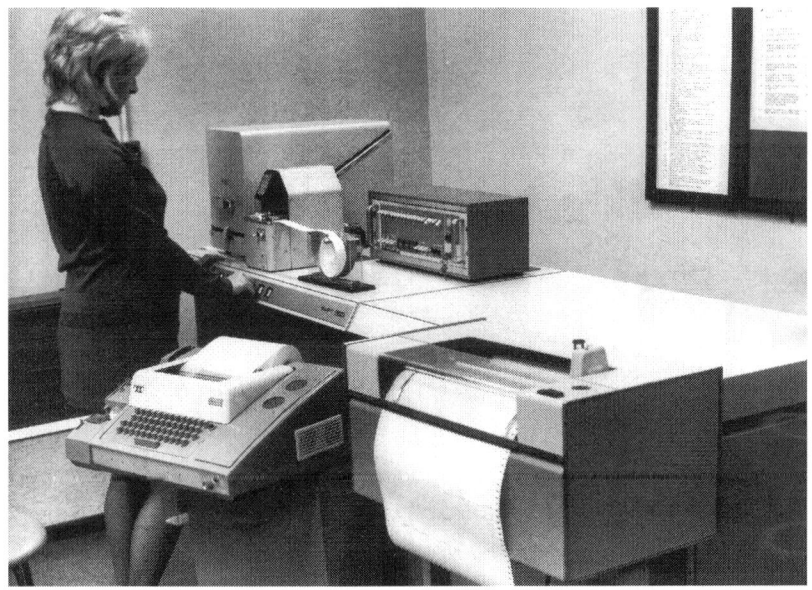

Fig. 113 WAI-1067-01: Elliott 903C Computer, 1965.

Main Lab L122 - Non Listed

Analytical services to Establishment.

The conversion and reuse of what had become venerable Victorian buildings into laboratories housing the most advanced research technology was an imaginative and cost saving exercise, in comparison with the alternatives. Adaptive re-use of industrial buildings has come to be recognised as one of the most important features of preservation of the national heritage. The Waltham Abbey Mills were one of the first examples and enabled the survival of what is an important centre of technological heritage.

The high quality and innovative research carried out in the laboratories produced novel technologies which were developed into manufacturing processes widely adopted by the Royal Ordnance factories and private industry.

Other Cordite Related Listed Buildings

"No undue haste must ever be made and no greater force applied than is absolutely necessary."

(Royal Gunpowder Mills Factory Rule Book, 1884)

1. Safety - The Magazines

A number of other cordite related listed buildings were related to safety.

The phrase 'powder magazine' tends to convey an image of a substantial building storing large quantities of gunpowder, often away from the site of manufacture and often built in grandiose style symbolising the power of the Authorities. However a different type of magazine, of smaller size, performed a vital safety function within the manufacturing area.

Explosives manufacture was hazardous and accidents did occur. The story of explosives safety is one of a long progression from early attitudes which hardly took account of safety at all through arduously learned lessons to the stringent controls of today. A report of 1864 on conditions at powder magazines at Erith graphically illustrates how desperately control was needed - magazines not closed or guarded, doors opening directly on to a river bank with a footpath along which the public walked, frequently smoking pipes, the presence of small boys augmenting their pocket money by selling matches to the smokers, passing river steamers emitting showers of sparks from their funnels and to cap it all, the annual burning of nearby reed bed stubble.

Increasing Government awareness of the need for better safety provision within the gunpowder manufacturing process, including the need for more control over storage amounts and amounts held in process buildings, was reflected in legislation. Expense and Charge magazines were built in civil and governmental factories:

- Expense magazines for safe storage of product batches awaiting movement to further processing.
- Charge magazines for enabling control of the of the quantities being worked on in the manufacturing area by providing separate storage for incoming material until it could be moved into processing within the permissible limits.

The main legislation reflecting Governmental control of gunpowder and explosive manufacture, transport and storage was contained in Acts of 1719, 1771, 1772, 1860 and 1875. The first two Acts were concerned manly with outside transportation and storage.

The 1772 Act was the first to include regulation of activity within the manufacturing facility, introducing provision for licensing of manufacture, limiting the amounts of powder which could be processed at one time and laying down limits for material which could be held awaiting processing, minimum distance of storage buildings from mills and the materials to be employed in the construction of storage buildings. The concept applied to storage construction was opposite to that for manufacturing. In the latter a light construction was employed at various points providing a channel for blast away from adjacent buildings in the event of an explosion. In contrast storage buildings had to be of strong construction in order to protect the contents. By the mid 19th century it was apparent that the 1772 Act was failing - it did not cover new types of ammunition and explosives or processes and the mechanics of enforcement were lacking.

A particularly serious explosion in Birmingham in 1859 led to the Act of 1860 which covered the new types of explosives, in the manufacturing area amending the maximum permissible charge for incorporation, introducing limits for material processed in danger buildings and laying down requirements for Expense magazines. However in spite of further legislation to improve and extend the 1860 Act, it still failed to adequately regulate the industry. A whole series of explosions heightened public and Parliamentary unease - 1864 Erith, the subject of the report outlined above, 1868 the great Barnsley firework explosion, in one month in 1869 - Notting Hill, a guncotton magazine in Cornwall and Blackbeck gunpowder works.

Finally in 1874 there was the great Regents Canal explosion in which fumes from barrels of petroleum on a canal barge were ignited by an oil lamp and caused 5 tons of gunpowder to blow up. This was no rural backwater but in the heart of London and attracted immense publicity. Major V. Majendie R.E., Inspector of Gunpowder Works, conducted the subsequent enquiry. Public opinion was demanding that something had to be done and Majendie made far reaching recommendations. The subsequent Explosives Act of 1875, including a licensing and inspection system, finally proved an effective and long lasting medium for control of the industry. Majendie's time had come. He embarked on a crusade to make the industry safer and could be regarded as "the father of health and safety". He was promoted to Colonel, appointed the first Inspector of Explosives and eventually knighted. Col. Majendie needed a very thick skin. The pillars of the Victorian explosives industry were not accustomed to outside interference in their activities and correspondence between them and Majendie has been cited as some of the finest examples in the

English language of venom concealed in the obligatory elegant phraseology of Victorian business correspondence.

Fig. 114 WAI-1557-01: Col. V. D. Majendie. Father of Explosives Health and Safety.

Fig. 115 WAI-0404-12: Monumentality of Gunpowder Safety. A brick rubble filled blast wall / traverse at Waltham Abbey, 1978.

Fig. 116 WAI-0330-01: The Cleaning Crew; essential to guard against build up of dangerous explosive dust, 1896.

The Listed Magazines

The listed magazines at Waltham Abbey include both Expense and Charge categories. Magazines were already in place for gunpowder and were readily converted to deal with the materials for cordite. As the Mills expanded with increased steam production so magazines proliferated, particularly at the time of significant expansion in 1878 when new moulded powders were introduced. There is a particular concentration across the Middle Stream from the steam incorporating mills.

An essential component of the 1878 expansion was the extension of the high level canal system and along with this a lock was built immediately to the north of the magazines to provide a connection with the lower level system and thus with the magazines.

Fig. 117 WAI-0404-18: North Site Canal Lock.

L133 Magazine, Built 1879 (Listed Grade 2)

This magazine, one of the cluster of magazines overlooking the Middle Stream, was converted to a Charge Magazine for cordite paste - the guncotton / nitroglycerine mix, prior to moving to the cordite incorporating mill.

Fig. 118 WAI-1585-01: Magazine L133, built 1879. (Photograph 2012)

L135 Tray Magazine, Built 1882 (Listed Grade 2)

Situated on the opposite side of the canal from L133, with porch protecting the canal side loading stage, this building is the epitome of the small cordite magazine and, in conjunction with the rounded canal bridge to the north, forms probably the most photographed scene on the site.

After extrusion cords of cordite were placed on trays and taken to this magazine for storage and onward processing.

Of particular interest is the floor covering of the loading area. This is the sole surviving example of the use of animal hide in the mills, kept moist to prevent accumulation of gunpowder dust, which could be ignited by a spark. The hide was fastened by anti spark non ferrous, copper nails.

Fig. 119 WAI-1585-02-01: Tray Magazine L135, built 1882. (Photograph 2012)

L141 Sorting House, Built 1889 (Listed Grade 2)

Originally a gunpowder expense magazine, situated at the north end of the steam mills, this building was served by the raised railway, with raised doors.

By 1910 it was termed Sorting House, associated with cordite production.

L154 Expense Magazine, Built 1864 (Listed Grade 2)

Lying to th north of Group C mills, this again is one of the surviving gunpowder expense magazines for storing material after incorporation. It made the transition to cordite around 1917 and was a store for material produced by cordite incorporation - 'dough'.

Fig. 120 WAI-1585-04: Sorting House L141, built 1889. (Photograph 2012)

Fig. 121 WAI-1585-09: Expense Magazine L154, built 1864. (Photograph 2012)

L170a Expense Magazine, Built 1857 (Listed Grade 2)

Lying to the east of the L168 Mechanics Shop, this magazine occupies a special place in the history of the magazines as it was built to serve the first steam mills, Group A, destroyed in 1861. It stored material after incorporation in the Group.

When Group A was built a tramway link, initially pushed by hand, was established to bring material from the mixing house. This involved raising the tramway on trestles to bring it up to the level of the incorporating mill floor, which was raised to accommodate the underfloor drive gear. The tramway was extended to the expense magazine which therefore has a raised door at the level of the tramway. By 1917, L170a was a cordite dough store.

Fig. 122 WAI-1585-14: Expense Magazine L170a, built 1857. (Photograph 2012)

L165 Mineral Jelly Store, Built 1917 (Listed Grade 2)

L165 rather improbably was built to hold vaseline (Mineral Jelly). However vaseline was an important element in the cordite matrix. The originators of the cordite mix included this material to prevent barrel fouling and corrosion. However fortuitously it was later found that the vaseline materially improved stability in storage - a significant safety factor in explosives.

Fig. 123 WAI-1585-11: Mineral Jelly Store L165, built 1917. (Photograph 2012)

2. Other Cordite Related Listed Buildings

Drying Stoves

L167 Reel Drying Stove, Built 1889 (Listed Grade 2)

After extrusion in the Press House the cordite cords were dried. This had a twofold purpose - removing remaining moisture and driving off the acetone solvent used in incorporation which would contaminate the final product.

For drying the smaller diameter cords were wound on to reels and the larger diameter cords were cut to the required lengths.

This building, lying to the south of the Group C steam mills, was converted to reel drying from its gunpowder function as a charcoal store, later becoming in the 1950s a Glass and Chemical Store.

Fig. 124 WAI-1585-12: Reel Drying Stove L167, built 1889. (Photograph 2012)

H7 Reel Drying Stove, Built 1904 (Listed Grade 2)

H7, situated by the main gate, is a good example of later blast protection design in which the building was sunk in an earth mound and thus only the roof and lightning conductors show above.

As cordite replaced gunpowder as the propellant of the British Forces, as well as extensive conversion of gunpowder buildings new building was required. H7 was part of the new building programme in the early part of the 20th century.

A tramway system served the building. This entered and left through a vertical facing wall with concrete revetments and these remain.

Whilst it was necessary to drive off the acetone vapour, this was a highly uneconomic process as acetone was a scarce and expensive commodity with various industries competing for supplies. In response on the South Site an acetone recovery system was developed and installed and the initial plant transferred to H7.

As in the technical field the Factory was in the forefront of safety development which fully reflected and was in advance of explosives legislation. The rush of the Industrial Revolution and beyond and the pressures of competition had meant that Victorian industry placed safety far down the list of priorities. The Mills attention to safety was part of the long climb to better and safer working conditions which took place in industry generally and in fact established a safety record superior to ostensibly safer industries.

Fig. 125 WAI-1585-21: Reel Drying Stove H7, built 1904. (Photograph 2012)

The 1787 Group

"In obedience to His Grace the Master Generals Orders, I Yesterday went to the Powder Mills at Waltham Abbey with Mr. Walton and had the said Mills and appurtenances thereunto belonging delivered to me for His Majestys Service."

(Wm. Congreve, Deputy Comptroller,
Royal Laboratory, Woolwich, 19 October 1787)

The 1787 Group

The three buildings in the 1787 Group are:

- A200 Walton House - Listed Grade 2
- A201 Mixing House - Listed Grade 2*
- A202 Saltpetre Melting House - Listed Grade 2*

Fig. 126 WAI-0178-01: View of the Offices of the Royal Gunpowder Mills, Waltham Abbey. Drawn by J. Bell, 1851.

The significance of this 1787 Group in the history of the Mills is:

- In physical terms these are the only surviving 18th century buildings and the oldest on site.
- Technically, they represented the start of a rationalised approach to manufacture introduced by William Congreve involving all stages of the process from purity of ingredients, precise measurements, close quality control, machinery improvement and economy of operation, progressively establishing the Mills over 200 years as leaders in their technology.
- The processes in the Group reflected the initial stages of production. Physically they were situated at the beginning of the chain of production buildings.
- They were among the first Congreve buildings.

These three, situated on the Square by the newest building - the Establishment Library and Lecture Theatre built in the mid 1960s, now the main Exhibition centre, comprise a grouping on the Island site where original materials preparation and composition or mixing took place. This continued after Government purchase of the Waltham Abbey Mills from the Walton family in 1787. The term 1787 Group has been applied as these structures were among the first which Major William Congreve (later Lt General) then Deputy Comptroller of the Royal Laboratory of Woolwich ordered to be built immediately after purchase.

Immediately following transfer of ownership of Waltham Abbey, Congreve instituted a programme of repair, refurbishment and new building. Many difficulties were encountered, including water supply where local mills were competing users and production did not resume until 1789.

Ultimately the programme had cost, including the purchase of competing water users - corn mills at Cheshunt and Waltham Abbey, the considerable sum of £35,000 and represented a significant investment, reflecting the importance placed by the Government on providing a secure and controllable gunpowder source. It seems possible that the realisation by the Waltons that the Mills were going to need this order of expenditure to retain their dominant position was an influencing factor in their willingness to sell.

When the Mills were purchased the manufacture of gunpowder owed more to alchemy than science. Control of the manufacturing process was loose and quality was a constant problem. Of particular importance was the need to obtain not only better performance but more uniformity and predictability. Without this gunners were operating more or less on a random basis.

Congreve was a visionary who saw that the way forward lay in scrupulous attention to purity of ingredients, precise measurements, close study of each stage of production to introduce improvement where possible and quality control in general. These considerations might now seem self evident and even simplistic but at that time what was needed was a fundamental change in culture and only a man of drive with ability to achieve strong control could achieve it. In this Congreve abundantly proved himself.

In 1814 William Congreve was succeeded by his son, also William, as Comptroller of the Royal Laboratory and therefore Director of the Mills. Congreve Jnr. continued the emphasis on quality control, precise measurement and machinery improvement. Of particular importance in this respect was his development of a powder granulating machine regarded as the best in the world.

A200 Walton House Built 1787 (Listed Grade 2)

This building is in the original Mills area adjacent to the exhibition centre. Initial materials preparation took place here prior to moving on to the incorporating mills on the Millhead Stream. One of Congreve's first actions after purchase was to have built here, either totally replacing an original structure or building on it, a two storey structure of two bays by one bay with brick in Flemish bond. The roof was hipped with pegged trusses and these trusses, with original carpenter's marks for assembly survive as part of the present hipped roof. At this point it would appear to have been some form of administrative facility, connected with the Master Worker, fulfilling the same function for the previous Walton ownership. It now has the title Walton House.

Keeping pace with the Mills development, Walton House passed through at least five further phases of construction to give it its present day appearance:

- Before 1821 - North side extended to create a third bay with two storeys.
- Around 1860 - Two storey wing built at north end of east elevation.
- Later - Two storey wing built at west end of south elevation.
- 1888 - Two storey wing built at south end of east elevation.
- Later by 1895 - Service tower added to this wing.

Not surprisingly, in view of the high water table and the large number of additions which have taken place, settlement has taken place. This is visible but to determine on which side is not as straightforward as it might appear. Certainly the north side has a considerable lean as evidenced by the sloping internal floors.

Fig. 127 WAI-1585-17: Walton House A200, built 1787. (Photograph 2012)

The building work reflected the progression of administrative staff and ranks. By 1807 the building was termed the Storekeepers Office. The Storekeeper and Head of the Establishment played a vital role in implementing the strategy of the Comptroller of the Royal Laboratory at Woolwich. James Wright was appointed to the post in1787 at a salary rising to £300 p.a. He was a man of considerable ability, administrative and technical, and played a key part in ensuring that Congreve's plans came to fruition.

Wright was assisted by a senior administrative officer, termed 'Clerk of Cheques' and in 1788 William Newton was transferred from Faversham and appointed 'Master Worker' at a salary rising to £130 p.a. Newton similarly played a major role in ensuring successful operation of the Government Mills in their formative years.

A plan of 1856 showing the uses of the rooms in the extended building illustrates how the Mills administrative machinery had expanded. On the ground floor were - Master Worker and Captain Instructors Office, Managers Room and on the first floor Clerk's Office and Superintendent's office.

Significantly by 1865 Walton House was termed the Superintendents Office. This reflected the increasing importance of the Mills following the significant investment of the late 1850s and 1860s and the need for what was effectively a Chief Executive to run the Establishment. Later the Superintendent moved to other quarters and by 1908 Walton House had become the Main Office of the Mills.

A201 Mixing House Built 1787 (Listed Grade 2*)

The 1787 Mixing House stands across the Square from Walton House to the north of the group with a small extension beyond. Its building number can be seen on the brickwork. The building cost was carefully calculated and recorded - literally to the last farthing - £239 13s 6 3/4 d.

The original part of the building has two timber roof trusses each with a tie beam, king post with expanded base and raking struts extending from three sides of the base. The building of a new mixing house was an expression of Congreve's concern for purity of ingredients and close control to ensure that his instructions for precise measurement of quantities were consistently carried out to achieve a uniform gunpowder composition consisting of a mix of the three ingredients, saltpetre, charcoal and sulphur, in the precise ratio 75 / 15 /10. Prior to mixing saltpetre and sulphur were refined and charcoal produced by wood charring. The charcoal and sulphur were then ground and sifted and the three materials passed to the mixing house where the necessary quantities were first weighed then mixed in the mixing machine.

After mixing the charge was sieved and bagged ready for passing to the incorporating mill. At this stage the charge was termed the 'green' charge.

As time moved on like many buildings on the site the Mixing House lost its original function and progressed through a variety of functions. By the mid 19th century it was a Powder and Barrel Store. By 1886 it was a Storekeepers Office and Store and by 1906, in conjunction with various alterations, it was being shown in plans as a Drawing Office, Laboratory Store and Visitor Danger Building Office.

In 1830 Frederick Drayson wrote a remarkably detailed treatise on the current operation of the Mills together with suggestions for improvement or new building where considered appropriate. Drayson's position is not entirely clear but the balance of opinion is that he was what might now be termed management trainee and this was in the nature of a dissertation. His submission included a series of plans and elevations of the buildings and machinery and contents and these form a valuable record of early 19th century manufacturing practice in what was one of the leading gunpowder production sites in the world.

Fig. 128 WAI-1585-18: Mixing House A201, built 1787. (Photograph 2012)

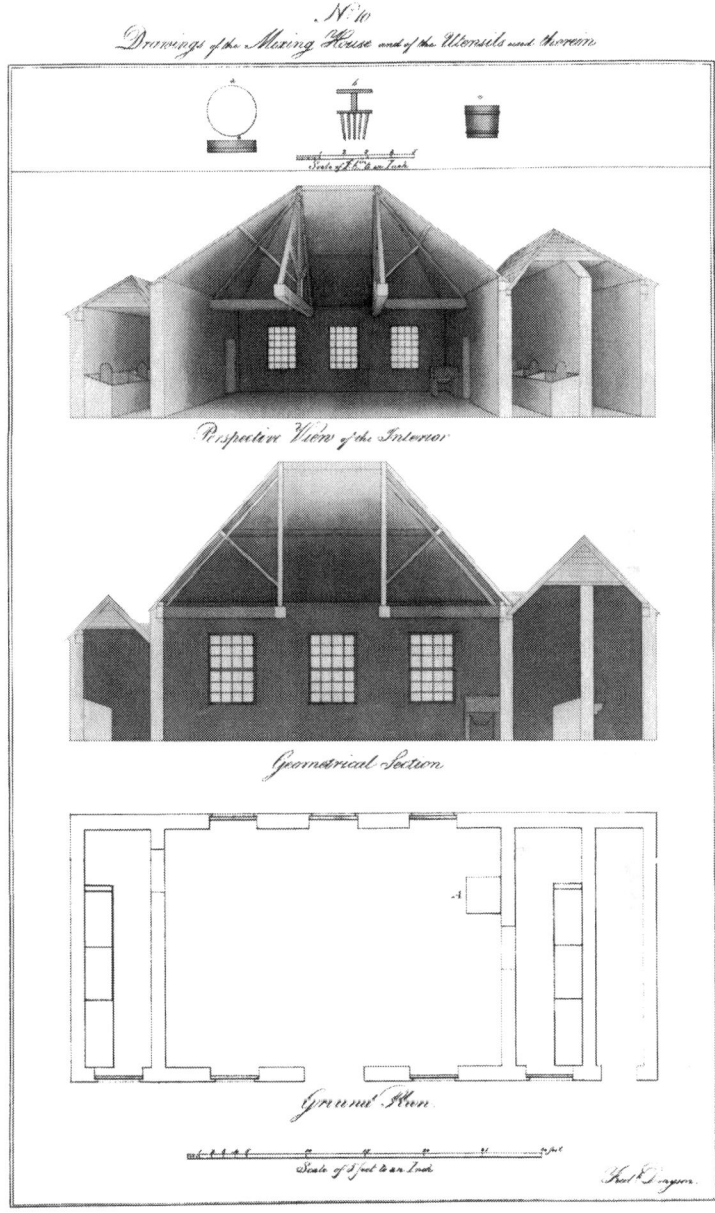

Fig. 129 WAI-0479-10: Saltpetre Mixing House. (A Treatise on Gunpowder, Frederick Drayson, 1830)

A202 Saltpetre Melting House Built 1787 (Listed Grade 2*)

Preparation of saltpetre took place in this building, linked to the Mixing House. Saltpetre was a fundamental part of the gunpowder mix and its condition significantly affected performance. Congreve therefore placed great emphasis on saltpetre purity. All saltpetre in Mills gunpowder was purchased from the East India Company facilities in Bengal. On arrival at the Mills it was refined in the Saltpetre refinery and then passed to the Saltpetre Mill for melting. The original refining method was to re-crystallize three times. Melting was intended to remove moisture and involved boiling or melting for two hours and then casting in moulds of about 38lbs. each. The resultant slabs were then packed into barrels for storage.

To ensure the best conditions for this last refining process, along with the new mixing house Congreve ordered the building of what was originally termed the Saltpetre Mill, later Melting House. The cost including equipment was £149 2s 0d.

The Saltpetre Melting House is immediately south of the Mixing House and was ultimately linked to it with a flat roof covering the link. It has a distinctive pyramidal roof and again has timber roof trusses comprising a tie beam, king post and struts from the king post base.

Later a new saltpetre process removed the need for melting and the Melting House passed through a succession of functions. By the mid 19th century it was a Wash Up House, by 1886 the Master Worker's Office, by 1908 the Cordite Foreman's Office and Store.

The significance of the 1787 group in the history of the Mills lies in the following:

In physical terms, they are significant as the oldest surviving buildings and the embodiment of structures of the 18th century gunpowder industry.

In technical terms, they represented the start of a rationalised approach to manufacture introduced by William Congreve involving all stages of the process from purity of ingredients, precise measurements, close control, machinery improvement and economy of operation, progressively establishing the Mills over 200 years as leaders in their technology.

Fig. 130 WAI-1585-19: Saltpetre Melting House A202, built 1787. (Photograph 2012)

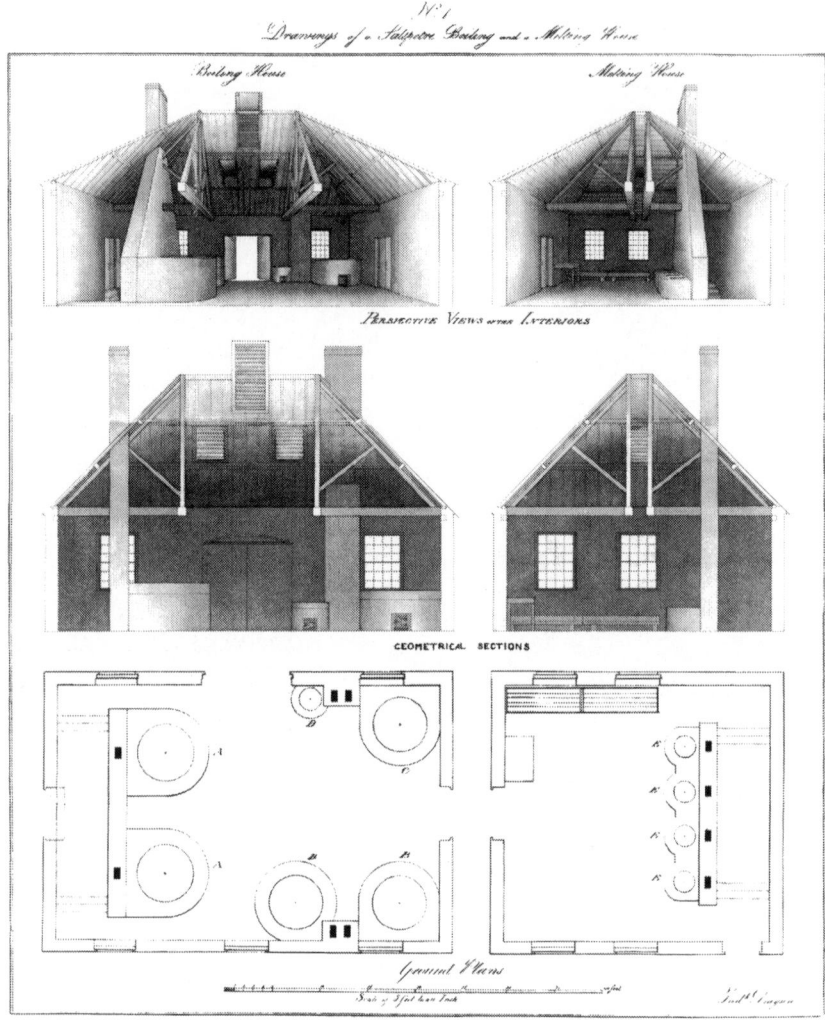

Fig. 131 WAI-0479-01: Saltpetre Melting House, on right. (A Treatise on Gunpowder, Frederick Drayson, 1830)

The Power Buildings

"I sell here sir what all the world desires to have - POWER."

(Matthew Boulton, partner in Boulton & Watt steam engine
manufacturers to James Boswell, 1776)

The buildings covered are:

- L136 Remote Accumulator Tower - Listed Grade 2
- L177 Dynamo House - Listed Grade 2*
- A221 The Lodge - Listed Grade 2

Power has been fundamental to all human activity, agricultural, industrial, social and over the years the Mills reflected the various forms of power as they developed from horse / water to steam to hydraulics and electricity.

Hydraulic Power

L136 Remote Accumulator Tower Built 1879 (Listed Grade 2)

This building is situated just south of the lock linking the high and low level water systems. It represents the large scale application of hydraulic power to the moulding operation.

Pressing and moulding both reflected the application of pressure power. In the gunpowder industry pressing was originally employed to re-work gunpowder dust. After the introduction of edge runner incorporation it was needed to press the looser millcake produced by the edge runners in comparison with the material previously produced by stamping. The process relied on muscle power applied to hand screw presses.

In 1795 Joseph Bramah patented his method of employing water pressure created by a hand lever as a pressing medium. Around 40 years later hydraulic technology took another step forward at the Mills. The hand leverage of the Bramah press was supplanted c. 1854 by the power of a water wheel to power the pumps in two new presses. The configuration was the same - pump separated from the press by a traverse. One of these presses with pump and water wheel still stands today on the eastern side of the site as a survivor of this form of mid Victorian hydraulic technology, possibly unique in the world - see Chapter 6.

Fig. 132 WAI-1585-03-01: Remote Accumulator Tower L136, built 1879. (Official Photograph 2012)

In an era of massive infrastructure projects there was a strong impetus for more power in all forms. In the hydraulic field it fell to William Armstrong to develop a system which represented a quantum leap forward - high pressure produced by steam driven pumps in conjunction with the weight loaded accumulator. Armstrong had successfully used steam to produce pressure via pumps for cranes, capstans, etc., and for applications such as dock gates had employed towers to hold a head of water sufficient to sustain pressure by gravity. However elevated gravity storage tanks were not practicable for large scale development. Due to the height and consequent high overall weight they required excessive foundation work and could not supply the higher pressures which were being demanded.

To counter this situation and make higher pressure systems practicable, Armstrong devised the weight loaded accumulator to regulate pressure, smooth fluctuations in supply and demand, and provide some energy storage. The accumulator was placed between the pumps and the pressure main. It consisted of a vertical cylinder standing in the centre of the tower with a ram supporting a crosshead. The crosshead ran between guides on two sides of the tower. From the crosshead was hung a weight case containing any heavy material available, e.g. ship ballast, scrap iron. A steam engine actuated the pumps to produce a store of pressurised water in the accumulator, topped by the ram. In operation, as demand on the hydraulic system arose, the weighted ram would fall in the cylinder, triggering the steam engine to reactuate the pumps to replenish the store with the ram rising. supplying a boost to the supply from the pumps, allowing the steam engine to adjust to the change in demand. When power demand slackened, the water from the pumps drove the ram up again. When the ram was fully raised, the steam engine would be shut off by a trip on the accumulator linked to the throttle valve.

Fig. 133 WAI-1602-01: W. G. Armstrong, Solicitor, prolific inventor and scientific researcher, father of hydraulic power, pioneer of hydro electricity, ship builder, and founder of engineering conglomerate.

Fig. 134 WAI-1656-01: Hydraulic Accumulator. (The Manufacture of Explosives, O. Guttmann, 1895)

The accumulator, with its relatively small capacity, was therefore not so much a large scale energy store in the sense that an electric accumulator stores it but rather a means of maintaining pressure in the hydraulic system, smoothing fluctuations in supply and demand and regulating delivery pressure. In a sense it could be viewed as the equivalent of the steam engine flywheel.

In the meantime from the 1860s advances in metallurgy - new steels and in engineering techniques enabled manufacturers to produce increasingly large guns which required larger charges. This however created a paradox in that the higher explosive force of pressed gunpowder in this quantity increased risk of damage to the gun. A larger powder grain size was needed to enable better control and slow the rate of burning. For this purpose, powder derived directly from press cake was developed at Waltham Abbey and were called pellet powders, as described in Chapter 1.

This led to the need for more powerful compression facilities, termed moulding. The new Armstrong system provided the perfect answer and when Building L149 (Chap.1), ultimately Group E, was erected in 1869 to produce pellet powders by moulding it incorporated an Armstrong weight loaded accumulator tower in the hydraulics.

The accelerating pace of armaments development brought still increasing demand for moulding facilities, both for Guncotton and from 1881 for the new prismatic powders. This could have been met by a number of steam engines to power hydraulic pumps distributed around the site - but this was not economic and would have increased the fire hazard from numerous boiler houses.

Again the solution was the Armstrong accumulator. The crucial advantage of a hydraulic system was that it had the capability of conveying power around a site via pipe, provided pressure could be maintained. The accumulator facilitated this vital role. 1881 brought the introduction of prismatic powders produced by a hydraulically powered moulding process and the L149 based system was extended to serve the moulding houses.

The Armstrong accumulator was an extremely successful device, with high energy efficiency - up to 98 per cent of the energy expended in charging being returned during delivery. It had been found that in such a system there was merit in including a secondary accumulator tower at an appropriate point. This provided a further balancing and regulating function and also improved response time - it appears it initially supported the hydraulic pressing of Guncotton, before the introduction of prismatic powders.

Fig. 135 WAI-0080-18: Image of Power - showing the distinctive hydraulic accumulator tower with the 1917 pump house on left and the 1905 electrical power house on right. These buildings are now a fine example of adaptive re-use as the headquarters of a firm which includes refurbishment of industrial buildings in it activities. (Photograph 1946)

In the 19th century era of massive infrastructure development the application of hydraulic power was virtually limitless - from all kinds of railway equipment, capstans, hoists, bridges, swing and lifting, lifts, jacks, cranes, flanging and riveting, metal working, materials testing equipment and so on. Not only did it power the infrastructure it was a major force in building it. For example, in building the mighty Forth Railway Bridge eight different types of hydraulic machine were employed, including a drill for punching 6 million rivet holes.

For a time hydraulics were a serious competitor for and in fact in advance of the nascent electricity industry, with several major municipal authorities installing mains supply and a private company, The London Hydraulic Power Company at its peak having over 180 miles of mains.

L177 Dynamo House (Also termed Switchboard House) Built 1902 (Listed Grade 2*)

This building was constructed in 1902 at the centre of the east elevation of the Boiler House L176 (Chap.1). As the name implies, its significance lies in the introduction of electric power to the site. It first appeared in the form of electric lighting in the late 1880s. Pre mains the electricity production source would have been dynamo. At the beginning of the 20th century in parallel to conversion to cordite electricity replaced steam as the power source. A Power House housing Bruce Peebles generators was built around 1905 to the south of the site, now in private ownership converted to office accommodation in another example of adaptive re-use.

In the meantime production by the old water powered mills on the Millhead had continued, concentrating on fuze powders (Chap.3). Water power therefore witnessed both the advent of steam power and its ultimate replacement by electricity.

A cordite reeling house L169 was built on the site of the demolished Group A Mills and it would have been a suitable use for electricity supplied from the nearby Dynamo House.

Fig. 136 WAI-1585-16: Dynamo House L177, built 1902. (Photograph 2012)

A221 The Lodge Built Early 19th Century (Listed Grade 2)

Situated to the north of the site flanked by the River Lea, this building now has the same owners as the Power House. Built of yellow brick with slate roof it is redolent of Victorian senior officers quarters in garrison towns, naval bases etc. There were various alterations and extensions, e.g. the front entrance porch was added around the middle of the 19th century.

Continuing the theme of power, if the buildings above represented the technical The Lodge represented the managerial. It was the Senior Officer's residence, ranging from Clerk of Cheques in 1821, Captain Instructor in 1859, Staff Officer in 1897 and after the Second World War becoming the residence of the Director after the site became a research establishment.

The technical history of the Mills is not only about explosives but also the spectrum of the other technologies involved in their manufacture. The power buildings reflect the trends in power technology in the wider industrial world, from water through steam to electricity. Further, the hydraulic structures represent unique examples of an often overlooked but historically important power source.

Fig. 137 WAI-1585-20: The Lodge A221, built early 19th century. (Photograph 2012)

Other Principal Structures

The Grand Magazine 1806, 1827, 1867

From the 17th century as nation states grew into major Powers increasing rivalry on all fronts - trade, diplomatic, political, territorial - brought with it an increased need for defence of the realm and projection of power to protect trade routes and overseas interests.

All this brought an increasing demand for gunpowder. The British Government had relied on private suppliers but the system began to show increasing signs of strain, both in supply reliability and in quality. In an endeavour to remedy this situation by direct ownership, in 1760 the Government brought the Home Works at Faversham under its control and in 1787 purchased the gunpowder mills at Waltham Abbey from the Walton family. William Walton had died in 1711 and his widow, Philippa, in conjunction with the rest of the family, had continued management up to the purchase. In a sense therefore the gunpowder mills were the first 'nationalised' industry.

Under the energetic leadership of Major William Congreve an extensive programme of refurbishment and extension was instituted at Waltham Abbey. In 1806 a new storage building, termed the Grand Magazine, was built. Prior to this the Waltham Abbey system had relied on small expense magazines and on going shipment to avoid product build up to any great extent but demand and production was relentlessly increasing and it must have been concluded that a central storage facility was needed.

The First Grand Magazine - Built 1806

Location / Security

For safety and security the Magazine was located at the furthest point on the north from the manufacturing facilities on the Millhead Stream, just south of the Hooks Marsh bridge on an island artificially created by three channels tapped off the River Lea to supply water to the high level Millhead Stream. The site was accordingly tremed 'Mgaazine Island'. It was therefore in a strategic position to control the inlet gates for water supply down the Millhead production line.

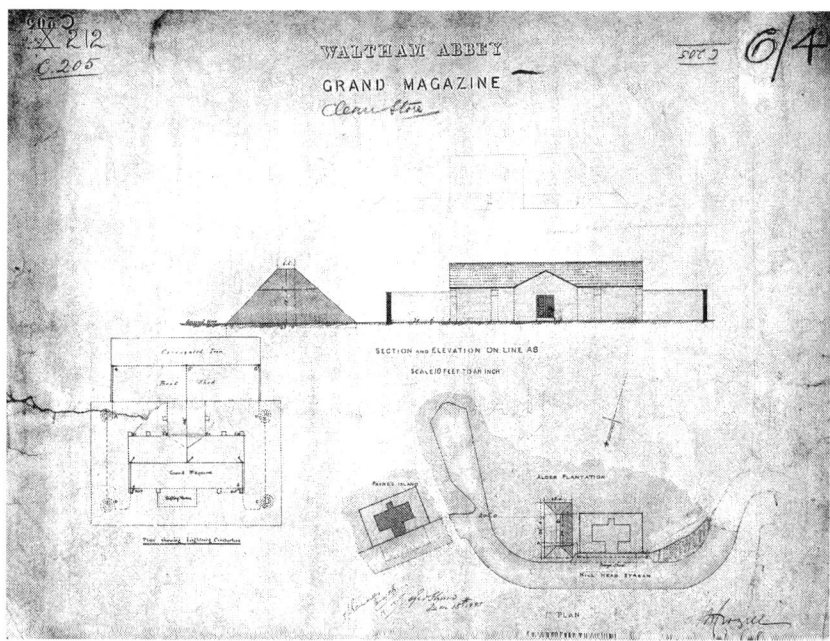

Fig. 138 WAI-1697-01: Grand Magazine Building 1, 1806.

For general security a Watch House for a warden was built, his duties including preventing any unauthorised person from approaching the magazine, preventing the carrying of guns across the island and prevention of any action which might lead to an explosion e.g. pipe smoking. The wardens were provided with pikes and sea service hangers - characteristic of security at the time at other similar locations e.g. isolated canal toll houses.

Function / Transport System

The Waltham Abbey system involved production on a batch basis with the gunpowder moving by water between the various processing stages moving from south to north up the Millhead Stream. The Grand Magazine in the north then stored the finished product allowing controlled loading on to and movement out by sailing powderbarges via the Powdermill Cut to the Lee Navigation and on to the Government magazines at Woolwich and Purfleet on the Thames. The barges were manually towed on the Powdermill Cut with horses taking over on the Lee Navigation and lower Lea after Bow Creek, where the Lea became tidal, and finally on to the Thames at Leamouth where sails were raised for the Thames journey.

Construction

The Grand Magazine was a plain rectangle 68ft. by 35ft., surrounded by a compound wall. The normal building philosophy for gunpowder storage buildings was to construct strongly of brick with vaulted roofs and buttresses to protect the contents from accidental explosion in adjacent buildings, the weather and in some instances from hostile bombardment. The first Magazine did not follow this, reflecting rather the light barnlike construction of processing buildings, with match board walls on brick foundations. It was presumably considered that its inland location, without nearby processing buildings made more expensive construction unnecessary.

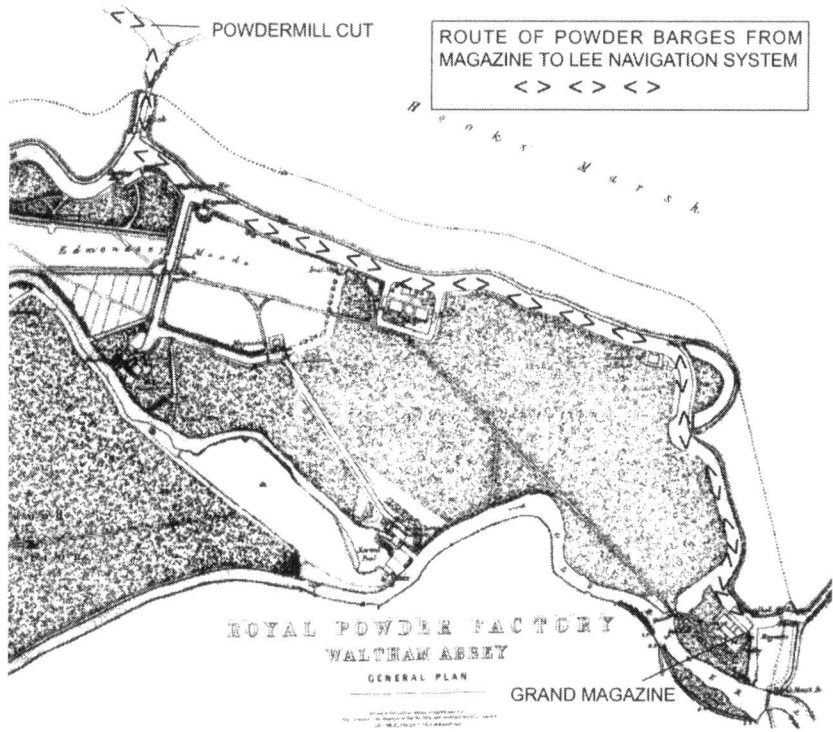

Fig. 139 WAI-1697-02: Route of Powder Barges to Lee Navigation.

Capacity

The Magazine held 1500 barrels - of a lesser order than the main Governmental stores - Purfleet, Priddy's Hard (4500 barrels), but sufficient for its function of storage / fairly speedy transhipment, whereas the destination magazines had to be large stockholders. The Magazine's capacity compares with the Mills output, which the 1801-1806 building programme had materially increased, rising to a peak of 22000 barrels in 1813.

In spite of its relatively light structure, in the organisational terms of its day the Magazine could be viewed as the fitting culmination of a period of improvement and expansion at the

Mills and an important point in a fully integrated industrial production, storage and transport system - one of the first in Britain and one which deserves a more prominent place in the economic history of the development of the factory system in Britain than it has been given.

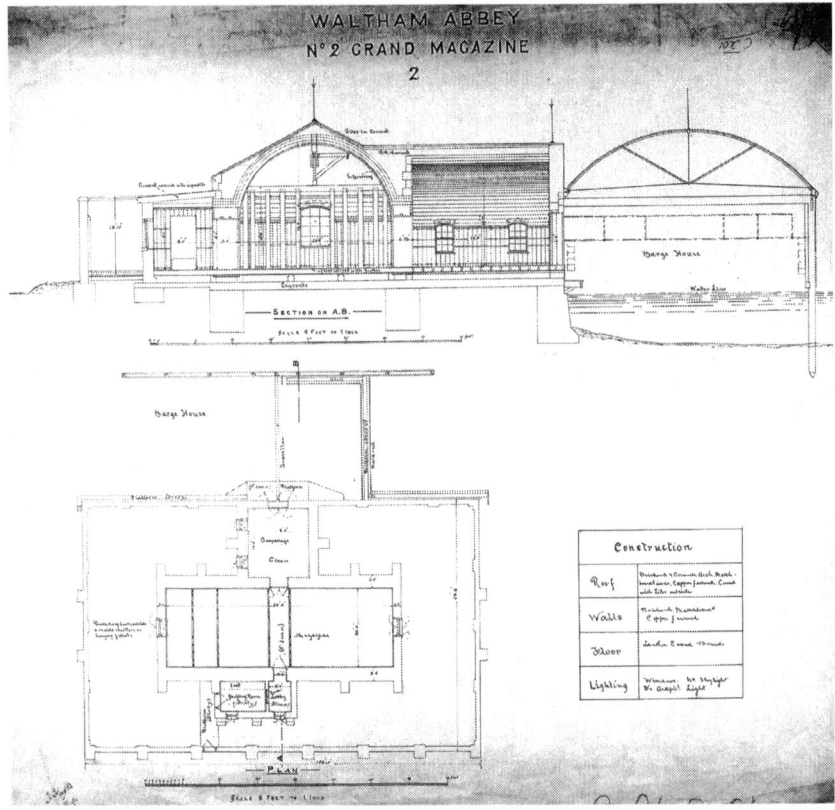

Fig. 140 WAI-1697-04: Grand Magazine First Rebuild, 1827.

Grand Magazine First Rebuild - 1827

The end of the Napoleonic Wars brought inevitable retrenchment, with a steep fall in production and staff numbers. However work originally planned in 1814, the year before Waterloo, did ultimately go ahead.

By 1827 the Magazine had been rebuilt again of wood and brick. The central rectangle was now 80ft. by 20ft. Crucially, loading facilities had been much improved by the addition of a barge shed and loading access bay on the west side. Later a belfry was indicated on the north side of the compound wall. The overall building shape had therefore moved from the pure rectangle to a cross shape and Magazine Island had become Pain's Island.

Grand Magazine Second Rebuild - 1867

Activity at the Mills continued at a fairly muted level into the 1840s. Events in the 1850s began to transform the tempo. Serious deficiencies in the British military supply system revealed by the Crimean War 1854-1856 and the Indian Mutiny just after reinforced the message that the Great Power status of Britain was on shaky foundations. Various military reforms were introduced and the Mills embarked on an extensive programme of modernisation, commencing with the building of the first steam powered gunpowder incorporating mills in 1857, followed from 1861 by the impressive range of incorporating mills on Queens Mead seen to-day.

The resultant output increases created the need for appropriate storage / transhipment facilities and in 1867 a second rebuild of the Grand Magazine was undertaken. The basic cross shape was retained. The central storage area was again rectangular - 65 ft. by 27ft. On the west side a projection contained a cooperage and on the east a lobby and shifting room and the building was enclosed by a compound wall 105ft. by 65ft.

Importantly the previous light wood construction was superseded by brick, with barrel vaulted roofs for the central area and the cooperage with buttresses supporting the weight of the slate roofs. The floor was of leather covered boards to keep down gunpowder dust and permit cleaning. Similarly the interior was lined with matchwood fixed with spark resistant copper fastenings. Partitions were inserted into the main range dividing it into four bays. In 1875 a 'traveller' was installed on the ceiling.

The barge house was iron built.

The spelling of the island had changed to Payne's Island.

Change in Function / Re-designation

Wet Guncotton Magazine - Late 19th Century

The late 1880s saw major developments in gunpowder technology to cope with larger gun sizes. However chemical science had accelerated to the point where it was able to produce more powerful and effective propellant.and in a remarkably short space of time chemically based material had replaced gunpowder as the military propellant.

The first successful chemical explosive, both for military and civil use, was guncotton. Later explosives were produced involving a blend of guncotton and nitroglycerine - the British patented propellant being named Cordite. At Waltham Abbey a guncotton plant was built at Quinton Hill on the South Site in 1888, followed by a nitroglycerine and cordite plant and in 1897 a further nitroglycerine and cordite facility on the North Site.

The Grand Magazine was now utilised for guncotton storage moving up from the South Site. and its designation was therefore changed to Wet Guncotton Magazine. It was transported in safe moist state. For cordite manufacture it had to be dry and guncotton drying stoves were erected on the North Site.

Building 2a Subsidiary Wet Guncotton Magazine - built 1915

Waltham Abbey was a main supplier of cordite to the British Forces and WW1 brought a massive expansion in output, from 26 tons per week to 140 tons. To cope with the increased guncotton storage requirement a secondary wet guncotton magazine was built in 1915 immediately south of the main Magazine. This was a wooden structure on brick.

The End of 150 Years of History - 1950s

Following the cessation of production at Waltham Abbey in the early 1940s the magazines fell into disuse. The subsidiary wet guncotton magazine was demolished in the mid 1950s and the barge house, cooperage and compound wall of the main magazine were removed over the same period, together with internal panelling and partition, leaving the central rectangular storage area which remains to-day. Later illegal brick removal left a gap in the wall.

Originally the roof and walls were lined with matchwood which was removed in the course of decontamination.

Storage - an essential link in the explosives chain

Explosives are hazardous - in manufacture, storage and transportation. The quality of the storage facility plays an important part in ensuring both safety and quality integrity.

From 1806 the Grand Magazine reflected the progression of the Mills role as the key supplier and developer of propellant to the Forces, firstly gunpowder then chemical base. As such it is a significant element in the storage aspect of the explosives industry.

Fig. 141 WAI-1697-05: Interior of Grand Magazine showing the results of illegal brick removal.

Fig. 142 WAI-1697-06: Digital Reconstruction of Interior of Grand Magazine. How it would have looked before the illegal brick removal.

Fig. 143 WAI-1613-01: The Powder Barge 'Lady of the Lea', survives today.

In the wider context the Grand Magazine remains as a reminder that from the deceptively tranquil location surrounded by marsh and water meadow flowed material which was a major instrument of the national geopolitical power, expansive or defensive, from the European conflicts of the Napoleonic era, imperial expansion and Pax Britannica, with the accompanying rise of the Royal Navy as a world Navy, and latterly two World Wars of national preservation.

Fig. 144 WAI-1697-05: The Grand Magazine, 2007. (Photo - Terry Griffiths)

The North Site Edmonsey Nitrating Hill 1897

The Grand Nitrator E2

In the forefront of the application of the new organic chemistry, in 1847 Ascanio Sobrero, Professor of Applied Chemistry at Turin University, in a letter to his old mentor T. J. Pelouze described his discovery of nitroglycerine.

Nitroglycerine was significantly more powerful than gunpowder and the possibilities of the product were eagerly pursued by the Swede Alfred Nobel who correctly foresaw its virtually limitless, and profitable, future as an explosive agent in mining and construction.

Initially nitroglycerine was extremely unsafe to handle but Nobel developed it with improvements such as dynamite and the creation of a safe detonating mechanism. One of his achievements, at first greeted with incredulity in the scientific establishment, was to demonstrate that the other major chemical explosive developed at the time - nitrocellulose, guncotton, could be gelatinised with nitroglycerine into a relatively safe product. Inevitably interest in the chemical explosives had been intense in the military field and Nobel, somewhat reluctantly, developed a military application - ballistite, patented in 1888. In Britain a year later a scientific committee headed by the Chemist to the War Department Frederick, later Sir Frederick, Abel in 1889 patented the military propellant explosive, cordite, based on a mixture of guncotton and nitroglycerine, similar in concept to ballistite but differing in quality of nitrocellulose, employing guncotton whereas Nobel employed collodion cotton, a difference which was later to have far reaching legal implications.

At Waltham Abbey land was purchased to the south of Highbridge Street, later termed the South Site, originally for

169

guncotton manufacture in a factory built 1888. Following this, in order to manufacture the new cordite, a nitroglycerine factory was erected on the South Site in 1891.

It was later decided to build a second nitroglycerine factory, this time on the original North Site, to the north in the Edmonsey area, completed in 1897. The centre piece was the 'Grand Nitrator' situated in the nitrating hill, Building E2.

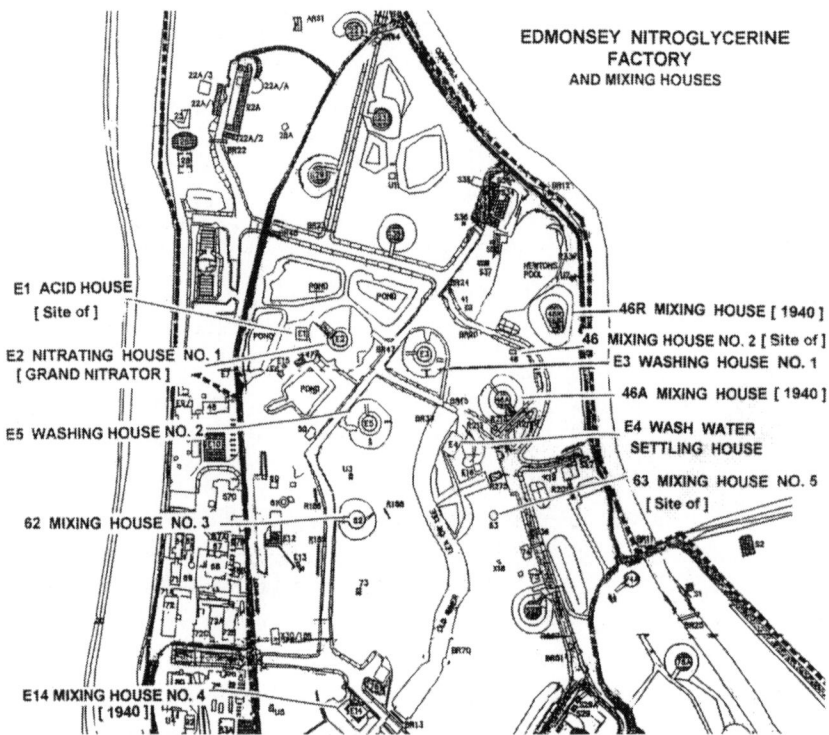

Fig. 145 WAI-1669-01: Map of the Edmonsey Nitroglycerine Factory.

Fig. 146 WAI-9101-01: Edmonsey Nitrating Hill E2, ca. 1900.

Fig. 147 WAI-1694-01: Edmonsey Nitrating Hill E2. (Photograph 2004)

171

Fig. 148 WAI-1691-01: Edmonsey Nitrating Hill E2. Entrance tunnel is curved to moderate blast. (Photograph 2004)

Fig. 149 WAI-1692-01: Edmonsey Nitrating Hill E2. Exit tunnel for nitroglycerine gulley from nitration area, floor removed, Drowning tank below. (Photograph 2004)

The Edmonsey nitroglycerine factory is now a place of mystery with derelict buildings in their protective earth mounds just visible in what is becoming a wilderness - a unique industrial landscape.

The fundamental element of nitroglycerine manufacture was that its explosive nature meant that it could not be pumped and the process had to rely on gravity to transport the product between process buildings, illustrated in the following process diagram.

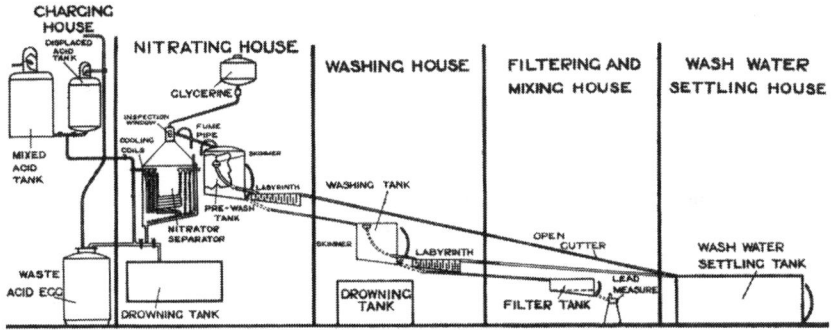

FIG. 54.—Nitroglycerine Plant (Displacement Process) at Royal Gunpowder Factory, Waltham Abbey.

Fig. 150 WAI-1637-01: Edmonsey Nitroglycerine Manufacture. (British Chemical Industry - Its Rise and Development, G. T. Morgan, D. D. Pratt, 1938)

A nitrating hill therefore had to be created down which the material could flow. Excavation for the hill produced ponds which were utilised to receive and render safe waste liquids.

The peak of the gravity flow was the charging house at the summit of the hill.

Initially acids and glycerine were conveyed to the charge house by lift but later this system was replaced by compressed air moving the material by pipe.

The hill contained the process plant, in which glycerine was treated with a mixture of nitric and sulphuric acids - nitration, in the nitrator to produce nitroglycerine. The acids were run into the nitrator first then glycerine sprayed into the base of the vessel. Prior to 1904 the nitroglycerine and waste acid were separated in a separation building but from 1904 this operation was combined in a nitrator separator.

Fig. 151 WAI-9157-B161: Edmonsey Nitroglycerine Plant showing the nitrator separator and the pre-wash arrangement, 1904.

Production was on a batch basis with the flow of chemical in lead lined V shaped guttering supported on trestles, with canvas covering fixed on one edge and tied on the other, permitting untying for cleaning and inspection after each batch. For safety each building was situated within an earth mound with the guttering leaving in a tunnel from the side of the mound, creating the unique appearance of explosives works with guttering connecting the various buildings.

After nitration the product moved down through various washing processes and then to the mixing house where it was mixed with dry guncotton to form a 'paste'. The paste was then blended with acetone in the incorporating house to form 'dough', which was extruded into cords.

Fig. 152 WAI-9143-192: Edmonsey Guttering to Wash House, 1903.

Nitration was carried out at 22°C. The temperature of the liquid was critical, If the temperature of the liquid during nitration rose above 22°C the charge was 'drowned', only a quarter turn of the control being needed to open the drowning stopcock releasing the charge into the drowning tank underneath, which was kept permanently filled with water.

The process demanded constant vigilance on the part of the operator watching temperature and fume colour through an observation glass and there is a famous image of the operator at the Nobel plant at Ardeer on a one legged stool designed to keep him awake or fall off! The idea was not new in explosives. One of the main applications for charcoal was gunpowder making. The old method of making charcoal was to make a kind of wigwam of wood, cover it with turf and set light to it to achieve the charring necessary for charcoal. If the fire broke through the wood would burn rather than char and the stack had to be closely watched. This was a soporific task similar to nitroglycerine watching with an equal risk of nodding off. To counter this the burner sat on a log set vertically on the ground with an effect similar to the one legged stool.

The quick access drowning handle can still be seen in explosives factory images half a century and more later

Fig. 153 WAI-1379-01: Ardeer One Legged Stool. (ICI Archive)

The Edmonsey nitrator had a fine safety record and as far as is known no charge had to be drowned. However the human element could not be left out. Glycerine injection was a critical operation and the rate of injection was subject within bounds to the attitude of the individual operator. Just as with steam railway engines some operators had a more dashing temperament than others which they expressed in the plant operation. One operator at the Royal Naval Cordite Factory, Mr. A. Webber, achieved fame of a sort when he was cited somewhat sourly by Dr. Ramsay, the Government Inspector commenting on irregularities in nitroglycerine factories, as a 'notoriously fast nitrator'.

The Edmonsey nitroglycerine factory and the Grand Nitrator within it were in the forefront of the development of industrial scale organic chemistry from the end of the 19th century in what could be called a Chemical Revolution with a whole range of products now regarded as essential.

Nitration was a fundamental element in this, both in military explosives and the production of chemically based products in the civil field and techniques developed at Waltham Abbey were widely diffused throughout military and commercial industry.

K. B. Quinan and The Quinan Stove 22a - 1936

The origins of the Quinan Stove lay in the rich gold mines of South Africa. Blasting was essential to mining, employing large quantities of explosives, which were a significant element in the mining economy.

Cecil Rhodes, in the shape of the De Beers Mining Corporation had come into conflict with Alfred Nobel on the price of his explosives and ultimately set up an independent company, the Cape Explosives Works. To manage it he recruited the American W. R. Quinan, manager of a powder company in California. In his turn Quinan recruited his nephew K. B. Quinan who became general manager on the death of his uncle in 1910.

Quinan was extremely capable and established a high reputation for the Cape Works and himself as an administrator and innovator.

War came in 1914 and by 1915 the British Forces were in serious trouble through lack of sufficient artillery ammunition and propellant. The Times called it 'The Shell Scandal'. Lord Moulton was appointed to head the Committee on High Explosives to reorganise and significantly increase the output of the munitions industry. Under conditions of extreme crisis Quinan received a telegram 'inviting' him to take up the position of Head of the Explosives Supply Department, charged with designing and overseeing the building of a series of factories which were to transform the munitions industry. The crisis was so acute that he was on the mail steamer from South Africa to London the next afternoon.

There is little doubt that it was due to Quinan to a significant degree that the Army ultimately received the quantity of ammunition it needed.

He was responsible for many developments to improve the economy and safety of explosives processing. The drying of guncotton to mix with nitroglycerine to make cordite posed a significant safety problem which also affected the economics of production. Guncotton was an extremely effective demolition agent for the Army and filling for mines and torpedoes. Part of its success was due to the fact that it could be stored and handled safely provided it was in a moist state and Waltham Abbey had a wet guncotton magazine for this purpose. However, for mixing with nitroglycerine to make cordite guncotton had to be dry and drying guncotton was a hazardous and costly operation.

One of the most significant expressions of Quinan's work was the giant factory built at Gretna, called the greatest explosives factory on earth and Gretna was a prime example of the use of a guncotton drying stove system which Quinan devised in response to the above problems, to become known as the Quinan Stove.

In 1935 it had become apparent that although Government policy was still one of appeasement to avoid war, there was an underlying consideration of what preparation would have to be made for war and the Government instituted a Committee charged with investigating possible sites for munitions factories and development. Within this programme authorisation was given for the building of a Quinan Stove at Waltham Abbey to reflect latest building practice, incorporate any advances in technology since the original design and gain experience in operation. The focus was primarily on the building of new factories in the west further from the possibility of air attack and the building at Waltham Abbey was intended as a template for transfer of technology to the new factories.

The Stove was constructed to the north of the site on the site of the previous guncotton stove No.17. It was served by a cut off the main waterway system. Two new boats were supplied with the description 'Dry Guncotton Boats - Quinan Type'.

External blast protection was in the form of 'Chilworth mounds', based on a design originating in the explosives works at Chilworth in Surrey, with earth revetted by bitumen covered corrugated iron sides, reinforced by flat bottom iron rails.

At the planning stage there was extensive consultation with outside bodies - to the extent that a model was constructed incorporating the latest ideas for comment by the Home Office Research Department, the Royal Naval Cordite Factory, the Chief Superintendent of Ordnance Factories and ICI.

Fig. 154 WAI-9248-01: Construction of Quinan Stove at Waltham Abbey, 1935.

Fig. 155 WAI-1693-02: Quinan Stove, 2008.

Fig. 156 WAI-1693-03: Quinan Stove, internal, 2003.

The 1930s were a decade of functional modernism in architecture and what emerged in 1936 was a building of decidedly modern appearance. Influenced by Modernism at that time, much experimentation was taking place in the use of concrete as a constructional material, extending even to housing. The new material was incorporated in the Stove in the shape of a semi circular cast concrete roof. Construction was on the Hyrib system with steel girders anchored in the ground interlinked with wire mesh rendered with cement. In the event of an explosion the design allowed for the escape of blast through a lightly secured roof.

The new building in its new material must have been particularly striking, even surreal, in contrast to the old guncotton stoves behind it which were rapidly becoming Victorian relics and today the contrast still exists, albeit with the Stove now itself becoming a relic.

Pre-Quinan guncotton was dried by fans blowing hot air produced in boiler houses. This was time consuming, expensive and unsafe. In an endeavour to improve the situation the amount being dried was increased. This in fact was exactly the wrong way to go.

The drying of a large quantity for a prolonged period of time led to super drying - continued drying after part is dry - this could lead to the highly dangerous electrification of the batch. Excessive drying times restricted throughput and increased utility costs. The handling of the material in large unwieldy batches led to the risk of friction which in conjunction with electrification could lead to fire and explosion.

Quinan had been aware of the problems and imaginatively turned the existing drying system on its head.

Super drying / electrification was avoided by rapid, 60 minute drying of smaller quantities in smaller containers at a much higher temperature.

Danger of friction at the unloading point was reduced by laying the material on a sheet in the drying basket with only sheet and contents being lifted out at end of drying. Warm drying air was conserved by a sheet of fine cloth over the contents of the drying basket.

The guncotton was cooled before handling by circulating compressed air through the material. The air cooled as it expanded.

Drying was done in separated bays with fire proof walls. To guard against build up of dangerous dry cordite dust and facilitate cleaning walls were lined with painted calico. In common with other danger buildings, lighting was fixed on the exteriors of the windows.

The up dated Quinan Stove at Waltham Abbey was a technical success. In 1938 it produced 177 tons of dried guncotton and it was reported that "the experience gained in operation has proved invaluable in the planning of the new cordite factory" (which would have been ROF Bishopton, Renfrewshire).

In a history of Chemical Engineering published by the American Chemical Society an article appeared entitled *The Role of Chemical Engineering in providing Propellants and Explosives for the UK Armed Forces* and in it is stated:

> "The principle of passing warm, dry filtered air and forcing it through fluidised beds of guncotton restrained from escaping by covers of special fine cloth was a brilliant solution well ahead of its time. It probably

increased the output of the cordite factory by 50% by reducing the throughput time."

Quinan patented his system and licensed the engineers Fraser and Chalmers Ltd. to manufacture and sell it.

At a time of two World Wars with explosives production crucial the Quinan Stove made an important contribution to productivity and safe working. Later technology moved on and the need for dry guncotton was eliminated by the wet mix process for cordite using a wet guncotton slurry. However this does not detract from the importance of the Quinan Stove.

Fig. 157 WAI-9251-01: Quinan Stove interior with drying tanks in bays 1936.

The Quinan Stove survives as an important and rare artefact on several counts:

184

- It represents what was in the context of the day a highly innovative explosives technology.
- A hidden example on a small scale of 1930s industrial Modernism utilising a novel building material - concrete.
- A reflection of the 1930s rearmament programme and a reminder of the political tensions of the time when national survival was threatened.
- Finally, it will serve as a forgotten memorial to K. B. Quinan, of whom the *Times* said: "It would be hard to point to anyone who did more to win the 1914 - 1918 war than K. B. Quinan."

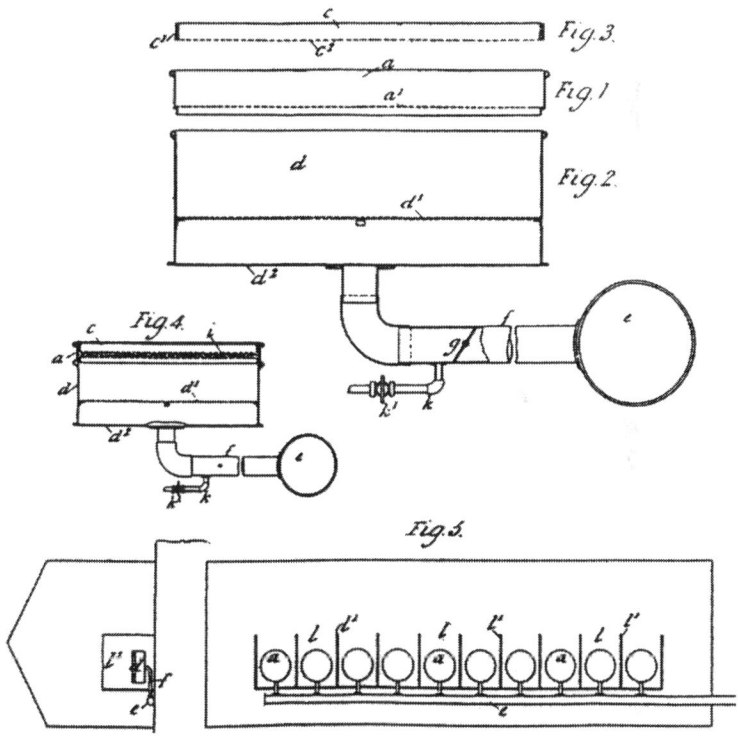

Fig. 158 WAI-0629-01: Schematic Diagram of Quinan System for drying Guncotton. Fraser & Chalmers brochure ca. 1936.

The Hydraulic Press 103, 104 - early 1850s

The inclusion of the pressing operation into gunpowder manufacture was a gradual process. Earlier it was rudimentary involving hand screw presses used to rework dust recovered from manufacture. Later as revolving edge runners replaced stamping, a mechanical mortar and pestle type arrangement, pressing was required to compress the millcake produced by the edge runners as it was of a looser consistency than that produced by stamping.

Technological advances led to machinery improvement and paved the way for the application of the science of hydraulics to produce the necessary power.

In 1795 Joseph Bramah, who had acquired an interest in matters hydraulic from his work installing the newly fashionable water closets for the gentry, patented his hydraulic press, comprising a hand lever operated pump and reservoir connected to a hydraulic cylinder and ram, based on principles enunciated by the French physicist B. Pascal. - i.e. the pressure in an enclosed fluid is the same throughout the system. This meant that as in the Bramah press in a combination of large and small cylinders with pistons connected by a pipe and filled with fluid a pressure in the fluid created by a small force acting on the piston in the small cylinder will result, as the pressure remains the same, in a large force on the large piston - multiplication of forces.

After improvement the Bramah Press enjoyed wide acceptance for "the throwing of small articles into bulk", particularly in the textile industry.

In 1811 a serious explosion occurred in one of the hand presses and a Committee of Engineers appointed to investigate recommended the adoption of the Bramah press, which would improve productivity and increase safety by the separation of the lever from the point of pressing. By 1830 there were at least 14 Bramah presses in operation at Waltham Abbey.

The advantages of the increased density produced by pressing became increasingly apparent - increased resistance to break up in transport, increased moisture resistance, more powerful explosive performance per unit volume.

After a period of relative calm after the Napoleonic Wars external international events and Great Power rivalry brought increased demand which began to outstrip the capability of the Bramah presses. Again the Mills authorities had to consider the need for a better and safer pressing facility. Having made one leap into hydraulics technology at the beginning of the 19th century with the Bramah press a further decision had to be made in order to satisfy increased demand.

Technogically Victorian Britain was seeing a never ending rush of new developments. Inexorably steam had made inroads in place of water as the prime power source. Iron was replacing wood in machinery and in construction. It could be expected that the any development at the Mills would include steam power. This however did not happen immediately. What was decided was to utilise water power in the form of the kinetic energy of the water wheel to operate pumps to produce the hydrostatic energy of hydraulic pressure power for pressing. Hydraulics had become increasingly attractive to the gunpowder industry. William Armstrong had introduced his hydraulic cranes and in 1850 had constructed the Grimsby hydraulic complex to power dock gates etc. Two hydraulic presses were built at Waltham on the site of old horse driven corning mills, consisting of press house to one side and pump house on the other, separated by a rubble filled anti blast brick traverse, with hydraulic lines connecting the two, with the water wheel to the side of the pump house.

Although the specific date is not entirely clear they can be placed in the early 1850s.

Why was steam not used? Perhaps a combination of factors - water power was readily available from the high level system and the Mills had long experience in operating it. Steam meant boiler houses with fire, a daunting prospect in an explosives works. An influencing factor could have been the available expertise of William Fairbairn's engineering company which was its peak in producing iron machinery and iron water wheels. Although the Fairbairn company records were destroyed the Waltham Abbey wheel demonstrates Fairbairn characteristics and there is mention of the supply of machinery to Waltham Abbey in a book written by Fairbairn.

The Hydraulic Press therefore utilised the latest water technology and the design was eminently suited to safe operation with the operator in the pump house being separated from the press house by the traverse.

Millcake was pressed on layers of copper plates in oak boxes. When the procedure was completed the boxes were opened and the presscake unloaded.

One aspect of the operation gives us a view into what was regarded in Victorian times as an acceptably safe procedure in gunpowder manufacture. In 1870 Capt. F. M. Smith RA, Assistant Superintendent at the Mills, wrote a manual of the manufacturing procedure. In it he describes the unloading of the boxes:

"Each plate, with a layer of hard slate-like cake adhering to it, is separated from the one beneath it, and being lifted into a wooden bin, gets a few knocks with a wooden mallet which causes the cake to fall off in irregular fragments, which are broken into pieces the size of a man's hand, shovelled into tubs, and removed to an expense magazine."

An innocent description, but containing the seeds of disaster. Sometimes the plates were difficult to separate and needed some persuasion with a copper chisel. In June 1870 a disastrous explosion occurred in a press house at the Lower Island works. It was concluded that a copper chisel had caused a spark by hitting a 'foreign body', possibly a grain of sand, in the presscake.

Only a few years passed before the Mills accepted the inexorable advance of steam, firstly to power gunpowder incorporating mills, then later to power pumps to produce hydraulic power for moulding. Ultimately with the introduction of chemical explosives a completete hydraulic distribution system was developed for cordite extrusion.

After demolition of the second hydraulic press the 1850s Hydraulic Press remains as the sole example on the site of water produced hydraulic power.

Further it is one of possibly only two remaining internationally, certainly in explosives production.

For many years hydraulic power was an unseen essential element in the operation of the railways, docks, harbours etc. The history of technology has not afforded it the recognition it deserves and many of its installations have disappeared or are not understood. The Waltham Hydraulic Press is an important and possibly unique example of a transitional phase in the history of hydraulics in a specialised application.

Fig. 159 WAI-0271-04: Painting - "The Gunpowder Press" by R. Tiniswood, 1981. From an original by an unknown artist.

Fig. 160 WAI-1667-01: Hydraulic Press. (Photograph 2012)

Fig. 161 WAI-0443-63: View of section of water wheel from Hydraulic Press interior control wheel, 1940.

Fig. 162 WAI-0443-65: Hydraulic Press Interior - pump, 1940.

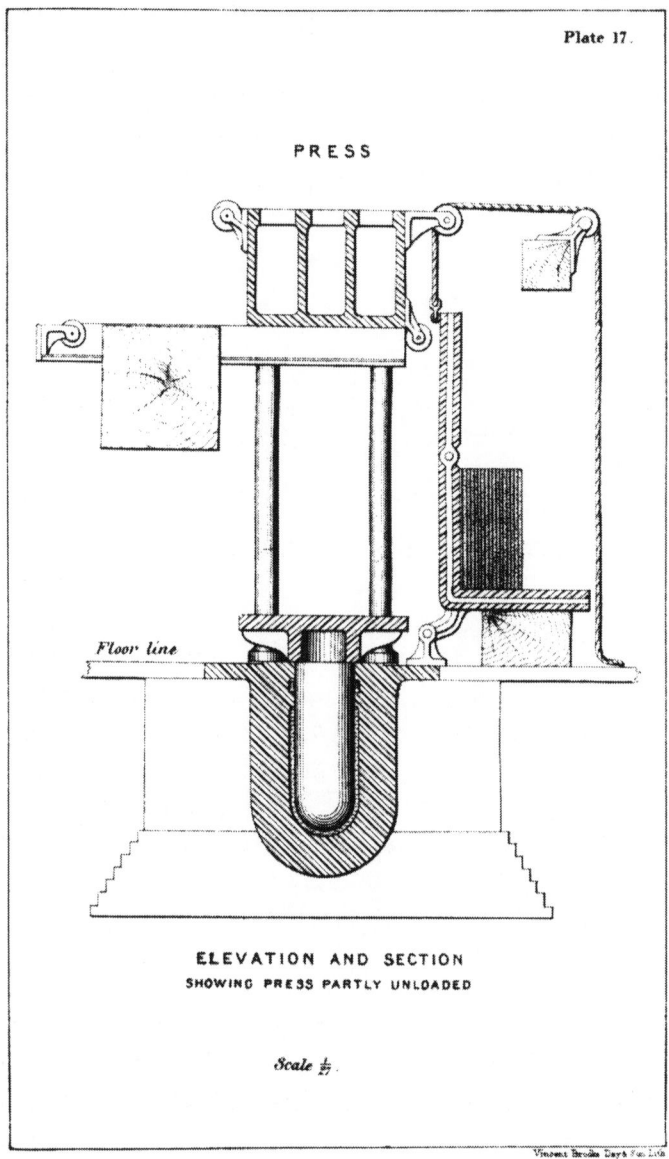

Fig. 163 WAI-0181-17: Press elevation and section showing press partly unloaded. (A Handbook of the Manufacture and Proof of Gunpowder as carried on at the Royal Gunpowder Factory Waltham, Capt. F. M. Smith RA, 1870)

The Main Laboratory - L122 - 1897

From the end of the 19th century explosives were in the forefront of the development of organic chemistry applied on an industrial scale. This gave rise to the establishment of scientific laboratories in which the new products and procedures could be tested and developed.

At Waltham Abbey following the construction of the guncotton, nitroglycerine and cordite factories the need for a rationalised central laboratory was soon apparent and the Main Laboratory was built in 1897, later extended in 1902 - 1903.

Like the Quinan Stove, the Main Laboratory, situated at the north end of the Queens Mead, adds another, somewhat startling, style to the rich architectural mix of the Mills. It is two storey with exposed structural timber frame with brick infill, the exposed timber giving it the air of mock Tudor - not the style one would expect from a building which represented in its day the modernity of the new science. It could even be said that there is a nod in the direction of the Arts and Crafts movement, at that time at the height of its influence, ironically the very antithesis of industrial science. Whatever was in the architect's mind the Laboratory is an unexpected sight in the context of the Victorian grandeur of the incorporating mills and the mysterious disappearing buildings in the alder plantations.

The early days of the Laboratory are strongly linked with the brilliant young chemist Robert, later Sir Robert, Robertson. He had joined the Establishment in 1892 and steadily expanded his mastery of explosives manufacture and characteristics to the point where he was in charge of nitroglycerine manufacture and then in 1900 he was put in charge of the Main Laboratory at the Factory.

Fig. 164 WAI-1681-01: Main Laboratory L122, built 1897. (Photograph 2012)

Along with the direction of the normal work - quality testing of production batches etc., Robertson conducted extensive research, mainly into the question of product instability. This was a major hazard of chemical explosives, arising either from traces of acid remaining in the cotton fibres after manufacture in the case of guncotton leading to potential ' hotspots' and explosion or decomposition in storage altering the chemical structure of the product again leading to potential explosion.

In guncotton manufacture nitration acid was removed by a process involving first boiling in water then pulping and then further washing. These operations were critical to the safety of the guncotton and Robertson built on the earlier work of Sir Frederick Abel to develop after extensive investigation an optimum boiling procedure involving seven boils - two longer at the commencement, the first with weak acid to hydrolyse unstable impurities the second neutral and the balance alkaline to remove the acids. This valuable development, published in 1906, became standard practice in Governmental and private industry.

Test procedures were fundamental to the work of safe explosive manufacture. Improvement could be possible only if the researchers had access to valid test results for the procedures under investigation. Robertson made a special study of the Will stability test for guncotton.

He followed up this work by modifying the Will test to adapt it to measurement of the rate of decomposition of nitroglycerine.

He discovered that nitrogen dioxide could be detected and measured in low concentrations in air. This was utilised to measure the gradual decomposition of guncotton at medium temperatures.

A major problem was encountered with cordite igniting spontaneously in storage. The Will test did not throw any light on the problem and Robertson developed a new stability test - the 'Silvered Vessel Test'.

He undertook extensive investigation into the calorimetry of the explosion of cordite, involving placing the cordite in a thick walled steel bomb immersed in a calorimeter.

In 1906 spontaneous cordite explosions took place in magazines in India. Robertson travelled out to India with Col. Nathan, Superintendent of the Factory, to investigate. The Silvered Vessel Test proved invaluable in comparing the decline of stability with the temperature and time of storage, leading to determination of the safety limit below which the test should not fail. Robertson and Nathan subsequently wrote an exhaustive report on the conditions of storage with recommendations for the preservation of cordite in hot climates. This remained a classic reference source for many years.

Fig. 165 WAI-0328-01: Sir Robert Robertson, 1903.

The India report represented the culmination of Robertson's tenure as Manager of the Waltham Abbey Laboratory. It had become apparent that he was destined for the highest positions in the Government explosives organisation and in 1907 as a stepping stone he was appointed to the position of Superintending Chemist at the Woolwich Research Department, with its ancestry stretching back to the Royal Laboratory of the 18th. century. WW1 has been called the Chemist's War and Robertson played a major part in enabling the Forces to withstand the onslaught. In recognition of this he was created KBE in 1918. Robertson retired in 1936 but returned to Government service in 1939 and continued to give valuable scientific advice over the course of WW2.

As with other Mills buildings the functions of the Laboratory rooms adapted to new developments. In 1918 an overview shows on the ground floor a Glass Blower's Room, a Gas Room, a Store Room, an Assistant Manager's Room, a Nitrometer Room and a CE Testing Room. The last is of particular interest as it demonstrates the importance of CE (tetryl), a booster explosive, produced in a new CE facility at the Mills, constructed urgently in response to the demands of WW1. The first floor contained laboratories with at the north end Balances, Extraction Room and an Office.

Continuous quality testing at the Main Laboratory was the bedrock of the preservation of Waltham Abbey's reputation as a world leader and whilst inevitably activity quietened after WW1 it still continued as the bedrock. In a climate of severe budgetary constraints, by the mid 1930s although still performing well the equipment had seen better days. The following extract from the recollections of Dick Doe, ultimately a senior process manager, written for Touchpaper, the Newsletter of the Friends of the Mills, sums up the situation:

"The Main Lab had electric lighting (DC) but he apparatus was all heated by gas - even the fume cupboard was powered by a gas jet burning in the exhaust flue ! There was no such thing as a thermostat and stability test baths were filled with constant boiling mixtures of glycerine / water fitted with condensers. Standard ground glass joints were not available and each joint was hand blown and ground by hand on a treadle lathe. Aperiodic balances were unknown and we used ' riders ' to obtain 3rd. and 4th. decimal places, even on the large balances in the old Gas Room which had capacities of several kilos and had been used to weigh bomb calorimeters in days of yore."

"In the Heat Test Room cordite was ground in a mill like a coffee mill but fitted with two hand wheels just like those in old fashioned mangles. Similar hand wheels provided the drive for the Vacuum Pump used in the Vacuum Stability Tests on tetryl and this was used in a small room containing baths heated to 120 1/2 C."

The staff must have been quite fit - *"Everybody rode bicycles."* No universal car ownership then, some cycling daily incredible distances.

All this was about to change.

Behind the scenes whilst the well meaning Mr. Chamberlain was assuring the nation that there would be peace in our time a programme of rearmament in case the worst came to pass was under way. Demand for the Factory's products and in parallel recruitment went relentlessly upwards. The Main Laboratory section of the Annual Survey of the work of the Establishment for 1935 - 1936, extract below, gives a graphic picture of the effect on the Laboratory and shows how in preservation of quality the whole process of manufacture was continuously and closely analysed. Also most importantly it indicates that the Laboratory was very much involved with special investigations. Random items taken from the list of experimental development work undertaken during the year demonstrate the versatility and skill of the staff. - experimental nitration of toluene, examination of corrosion of stainless steel by sulphuric / nitric acid, investigation of the cresol content of phenol samples, analysis of nickel gauze proposed for use in cordite pressing, tests of the resistance of blue bricks to the action of boiling acid, etc. etc.

Extract from Annual Survey 1935 - 1936:

"The activities of the Main Laboratory have been very greatly increased during this year by the rising output of the factory."

"The total number of routine samples analysed in connection with the inspection of raw materials, intermediate and finished products, was approximately 12,000 compared with about 5,000 during 1934 - 1935."

"The field of experimental and research work has also been greatly increased, both in amount and scope, and an unusually large number of investigations have been carried out into problems connected with the development of plant, processes and the general running of the factory."

"Notable lines of investigation have been connected with the resistance to corrosion of many materials of construction for plant for acids and explosives manufacture, new method for the sieving and washing of C.E., and the alkalinity of guncotton during processing."

"Plans were developed and prepared for re-arrangement of existing C.E. nitration plant, and the proposed new C.E. nitration plant was designed."

"A considerable amount of experimental and research work was undertaken for the Supply Board Technical Establishment, including several investigations on raw materials for T.N.T. manufacture, an investigation of the commercial processes for Carbamite manufacture, and an experimental study of the economic aspects of the present manufacturing process for chloraostic ester."

From its inception the Main Laboratory had provided an analytical service to all Branches. Post War this continued as a main function.

An important additional function stemming from this was the induction and training of scientific staff recruited as the research activity increased, many of whom ultimately progressed to senior positions, both at Waltham Abbey and in the wider Governmental explosives establishment.

From the early 1900s the Main Laboratory was the focus for development of the new chemical explosives and essential performance and stability test procedures.

Since the days of the first William Congreve quality had been of the essence at Waltham Abbey. To maintain quality there had to be effective monitoring of the production. Throughout the life of the Factory this was achieved by the high quality analytic service provided by the Laboratory.

In parallel the Laboratory carried out many special investigations, leading often to valuable improvements over the whole scientific and manufacturing activity of the Establishment.

Fig.166 WAI-1486-01: (next page) Main Laboratory Staff, with Factory Superintendent (centre), October 1943. Possibly taken to mark the end of guncotton and cordite production in 1943 (tetryl was produced until 1944).

Appendix 1: Listed Buildings

Grade 1	L157 Group C Incorporating Mill (1861)	LBS No. 352172
Grade 2*	A201/A202 Mixing House & Saltpetre Mill (1787)	LBS No. 352176
Grade 2*	L148 Group G Incorporating Mill No.7 (1888)	LBS No. 433792
Grade 2*	L149 Group E Incorporating Mill No.3 (1869)	LBS No. 433793
Grade 2*	L153 Group D Incorporating Mill No.8 (1867)	LBS No. 433795
Grade 2*	L168 Engine House & Mechanics Shop (1857)	LBS No. 433790
Grade 2*	L176/L177 Boiler House & Dynamo House (1857 & 1902)	LBS No. 352175
Grade 2	L133 Magazine (1879)	LBS No. 352185
Grade 2	L135 Tray Magazine (1882)	LBS No. 352184
Grade 2	L136 Remote Accumulator Tower (1879)	LBS No. 352183
Grade 2	L141 Sorting House (1889)	LBS No. 352173
Grade 2	L145 Group F Incorporating Mill No 6 (1878)	LBS No. 433797
Grade 2	L154 Expense Magazine (1864)	LBS No. 352174
Grade 2	L165 Mineral Jelly Store No.2 (1916)	LBS No. 352182
Grade 2	L167 Reel Drying Stove (1889)	LBS No. 352181

Grade 2	L170a Expense Magazine (1857)	LBS No. 352177
Grade 2	A200 Walton House (1787)	LBS No. 352178
Grade 2	H7 Reel Drying Stove (1904)	LBS No. 352179
Grade 2	A221 The Lodge (early 19th century)	LBS No. 352180

Appendix 2: Site Map

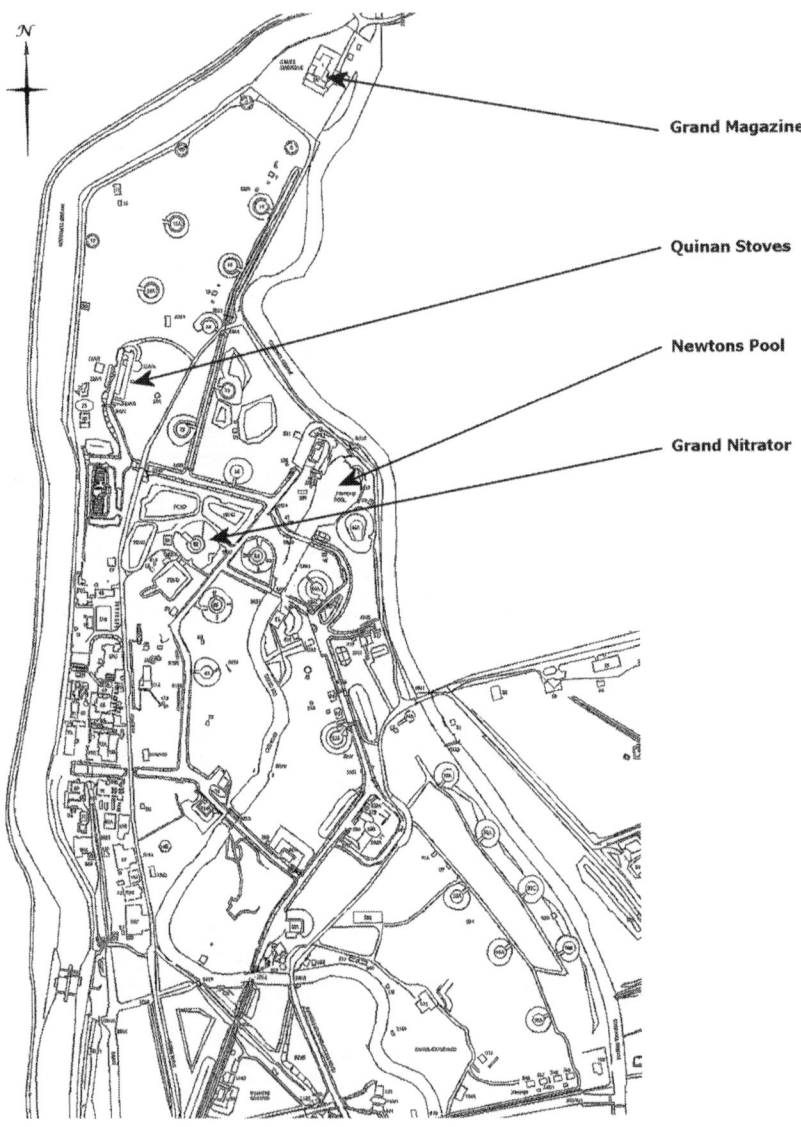

Site Map of the Royal Gunpowder Mills, Waltham Abbey - Top Half

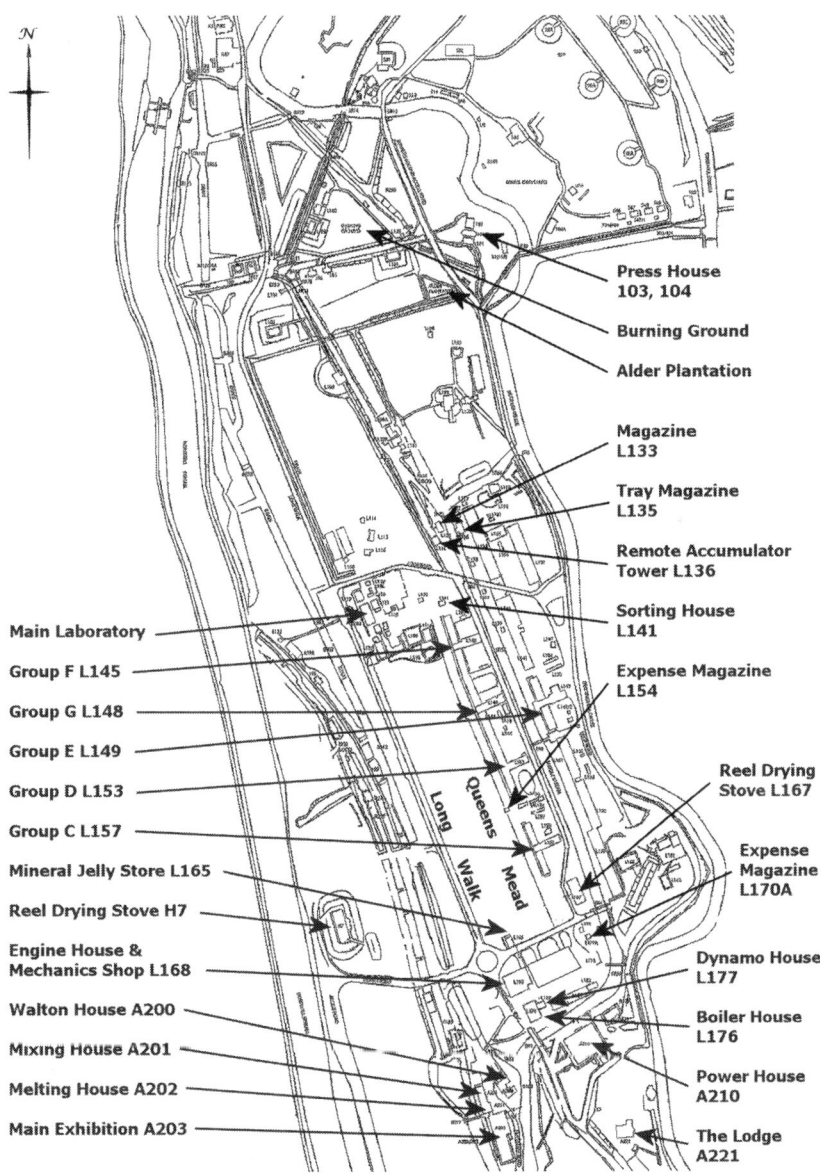

Site Map of the Royal Gunpowder Mills, Waltham Abbey – Bottom Half

About the Author

Whilst pursuing a commercial career in the oil industry Les Tucker became interested in the history and archaeology of the little known UK onshore oil fields.

This expanded into an interest in industrial archaeology and the history of science and technology generally.

He was able to apply this practically whilst participating in canal restoration work, combining study of the archaeology of canals with the history of canal ports and trade patterns on the canals.

This was combined with an industrial archaeology diploma course at Birkbeck, London University.

On retirement he became aware of the waterway system of the Royal Gunpowder Mills and the wide range of surviving buildings and technologies and pursuing this interest joined the "Friends Association of the Mills".

Today Les is an Archive volunteer at the Gunpowder Mills and his main role is Archivist for the Mills vast collection of documents and images and maps and plans.

During this time he has regularly contributed Archive related articles to *Touchpaper*, the Newsletter of the Friends Association.

He wrote the first Friends publication - *The Listed Buildings at the Royal Gunpowder Mills* and this publication is now an expanded version of that booklet.

7318384R00115

Printed in Great Britain
by Amazon.co.uk, Ltd.,
Marston Gate.